HOTEL ZYMOGLYPHIC

Jason Squamata

© 2019 by Jason Squamata and Jim Stewart
Illustrations, cover, and book design by Jim Stewart
Published by the Zymoglyphic Museum Press

The Zymoglyphic Museum Press issues a variety of publications related to the museum and its mission, including books. pamphlets, and zines. For the full list of ZMP publications, see zymoglyphic.org/pubs.html.

Foreword

In the fall of 2018, the Zymoglyphic Museum sent its resident scribe, Jason Squamata, a.k.a the Orakuloid, on a two month solo expedition to the fabled Zymoglyphic region. His mission was to penetrate its enigmatic fogs and bring back hitherto unknown insights about that mystery-enshrouded land that have up to now evaded the museum's researchers. He became so entangled in its multidimensional miasma that he has yet to find his way back. We believe he may have gone native. Fortunately, we have been able to acquire his journal entries via special envoy.

This is his report so far.

It must be noted that the existential peculiarities of the region are such that describing it using any known style of journalism or anthropological analysis is simply inadequate. Our reporter has given us a whirling verbal kaleidoscope to match the challenge. There are hints of the eternal epic poetry of Dante, glimpsing and pursuing blurry visions of his Beatrice in the mist, seen at times through a contemporary black-and-white film noir lens. The narrative morphs into a nonlinear "sentient liquid" of language, more immersive than propulsive.

Dive in.

Jim Stewart
The Zymoglyphic Museum

Foreword 3

PART I

1. THE HEARTBREAK INSTALLATION. 11
2. THE CONNOISSEUR. 12
3. MY ZYMOGLYPHIC YOUTH. 13
4. INCONGRUENT ORIGINS. 14
5. SECRET AUCTIONS. 15
6. ISOMORPHIC PSYCHODRAMA #9. 16
7. SLEEK AND ANEMIC. 17
8. MUSEUMS WITHIN MUSEUMS. 18
9. LET SLIP THE GRIP OF REASON. 19
10. ZYMOGLYPHIC DEMIMONDE. 20
11. DREAM PURGE. 23
12. CLOSING EVERY WORMHOLE. 24
13. IT ALL WENT WRONG, SOMEHOW. 25
14. DJ HOUSE FUNGUS. 26
15. ZYMOGLYPHIC NIGHTLIFE. 28
16. DEGRADATION OF THE TERRITORY. 30
17. CHASING TRACES OF IMPOSSIBLE PLACES. 32
18. HOME OF ALL HEARTS OR HONEYTRAP?. 34
19. THE HUNGRY JUNGLE. 36
20. A MUSEUM OF US. 37
21. THEIR LANGUAGE IS ALIVE. 38
22. DESPERATE SIGNAL/SECRET LOVER. 40
23. AFTER THE ACCIDENT. 43
24. RAINBOW BOMB. 44
25. I WOULD DO IT WRONG AGAIN. 46
26. THE DARKEST CONTINENT. 47
27. A SUMMER IN EVERY KISS. 48
28. I TOOK OFF MY GASMASK. 49

29. FEED ME TO THE SPIDER QUEEN........................ 50
30. THE SOCIETY IN SHAMBLES........................... 52
31. BUGHOUSE PHILOSOPHY............................... 53
32. HOW MANY MADE IT BACK?............................ 54
33. REPORTING BACK TO THEE............................ 55

Part II

34. REMAINS OF A ZYMONAUT............................. 59
35. HAUNTED BY THE GHOST OF ALL THAT ISN'T........... 61
36. SENTIENT LIQUID................................... 62
37. METACOSMOPHILIA................................... 64
38. CLASSICAL DECOMPOSER.............................. 66
39. OOZE 2 OOZE....................................... 67
40. SHE STARTS YOU OVER............................... 68
41. TWO AGAINST ENTROPY............................... 69
42. WEBS OF WORSHIP................................... 70
43. ZYMOGLYPHIC APPETITES............................. 72
44. THE ENDLESS REFLECTION............................ 74
45. AMBIENT SURGERIES................................. 76
46. LIMINAL THINGS.................................... 78
47. WEARING WOMEN..................................... 79
48. THE LAST MUSEUM................................... 80
49. DIRTY LITTLE MICROCOSMS........................... 81
50. PRIMORDIAL DESIGN................................. 82
51. SPECTRE COLLECTOR................................. 84
52. PENTECOSTAL LIGHTNING............................. 85
53. SHRED THAT MEMBRANE............................... 86
54. UNDISCLOSED FECUNDITY............................. 87
55. SCURVYSCAPE....................................... 88
56. A PLAGUE OF PILGRIMS.............................. 89
57. PAGES, FRAMES, & BUBBLES.......................... 90

58. PSYCHOPOMP AND CIRCUMSTANCE.. 93
59. CRACKPOT EVANGELIST. 94
60. DYNAMIC TENSION. 96
61. DREAM DISEASE. 98
62. FICTOPLASM JUNKIE. 99
63. THE GARDEN OF FORKING FAITHS (part one). 100
64. GARDEN OF FORKING FAITHS (part two). 101
65. EGREGORE. 102
66. THE CONCIERGE. 104

Part I:
Cantos 1-33

1. THE HEARTBREAK INSTALLATION

There's a kind of man you meet in bars
drinking by himself, consumed by regrets
and squandered opportunities, sometimes sobbing,
mostly just staring wistfully into the middle distance
as if all of his possible futures have imploded into a futile singularity
and he's watching it throb
you might spot this type at a bus depot or in a library
or shambling on a streetcorner,
wondering where and when it all went sideways,
muttering cryptic wards against the imperceptible pranasites that afflict him.
Your instinct might be to avert your gaze,
Knowing intuitively that the problems this ragged citizen wrestles with
are cosmic problems, and beyond your ken.
You wouldn't know where to begin.
But when you spot such a husk in a museum of all places,
An oddly haunted serene little secret museum like THIS,
occupied by a forgotten man who is quaking histrionically,
or just lingering too long at a certain diorama.
Consumed by its secret meanings.
By its urgent personal meanings.
You might feel his obsession eating all the energy in the room.
Even if you avert your gaze, your good time in this nice place might be ruined
by the shuddering proximity of a troubled man
who seems to be enjoying the museum a little too much.
Or maybe you're the pensive type, not so prone to outrage.
Maybe you'll just silently speculate, like the broken stranger
is a part of the museum and its mesh of meanings.
You'll maybe wonder what kind of crooked road
could lead a man to a moment like this…every other Sunday.
You might ask him why he's always here. What wounded him?
And how do these bizarre assemblages of objects speak to his tragedy?
He might stare through you at first, like his gaze is trained
on horizons you don't have the apparatus to perceive
and he must adjust his focus. And it's like you've never asked.
And it's like he doesn't know you. And he gives a different answer every time.

2. THE CONNOISSEUR

I guess you could say that I've always been a connoisseur of liminal spaces.
Interstitial crepuscular quadrants where the physics are ambiguous and the rules of either/or do not apply.
No point of origin could explain me to myself, no destination satisfy my hunger for becoming.
So my soul flows towards the crossroads, to crooked rooms between the scenes where the soul breaks character and rehearses all that is to come as the angels shift the subtext and the lighting.
I came scrabbling out of nowhere like so many, and that maybe makes it easy, letting slip the grip of reason and listening under every wind for a lonesome hobo harmonica or the manic pipes of Pan.
Taking to the night roads with the winged dust at the slightest provocation.
There are aristocrats in our tribe, defrocked mostly, but when Otherness calls you like a priest is called, no kind of cozy can hold you. All the gilded lilies, just dust when you touch them. All the big city bright lights flicker and dim.
The world as anatomized in conventional encyclopedias is full enough of wonders to slake the thirsty minds of most. But for we desperate few, we who go everywhere and nowhere at once, we who have glimpsed the tacky sideshow machineries behind the scrim of sloppy substance, there's a state of mind that is also a place and, dare I say it, a state of grace, a rich abyss that sings us home as if it's where we come from.
The first fragile notes might reach you through a poem or an accident or an umbrella placed with menace beside a sleek, defenseless sewing machine on a recreational dissecting table.
Any arrangement of objects that seems to obliquely evoke a shaping eye in the mess of thing, any shrill synchronicity that burns you with its urgency without overtly disclosing its significance, any moment that makes you wonder which dream you went to sleep in...these are the vectors through which a sophisticated Otherness enthusiast is led from the vaguely mystical and the amorphously occult to the Zymoglyphic. The museum. The mythology. The way of seeing.
I was barely a person to start with, it's true, but it took this curious cabinet of alien ephemera to mess me up and thrill me forever.

3. MY ZYMOGLYPHIC YOUTH

I've compared notes with those who are also afflicted.
Sometimes it's a shadow that lingers just a breath too long on the wall.
Sometimes it's a psyche-splitting frequency that speaks urgently in a language we lack the organic apparatus to receive.
An alien breeze unsettling the trees in a waiting room painting.
A subway glimpse of an unknown foreign currency that you've only seen and spent in dreams. A sentence that slithers with malevolent intent. A paragraph that makes you taste it. Every page a bolus of strange solicitations.
A scene in a film that makes it seem like there are things that can be known, that something is real out there, amongst the screens.
You connect the dots. Each dot representing a moment when you felt truly and deeply alive.
Always a moment when everything you know seems about to unfold into something else entirely.
A howling doorway. A playground at dusk.
Autumnal strains on a distant piano.
An understanding in the marrow of your crystal body of those who burned before you with the same bits missing as you.
Knowable only in flashes through the trances and incantations
of those who burned before me, those unholy men and women and otherlings with the same bits missing as me, those who tugged at the veil so recklessly
Homesick for the vistas of a chaotic eternity.
Changeling syndrome, afflicting many gifted children.
Many lost and squandered souls, others always about to go missing.
If the mists conspire to consume us and the stars abet them in their yearning, we find our way after much wandering to one of these museums.
Fewer and fewer since the accident, but each a way through, unless you've sinned against the territory. Unless the mist won't have you.
You start catching references to the Zymoglyphic in radio chaos and the schizoid scripture of street people.
You follow phantom footsteps from rabbit hole to rabbit hole.
Finding at last that there is a word for this shiver that afflicts you when expired timespace decays into everywhen. A word for this feeling, this calling A word for where it comes from. A word for where we are going.

4. INCONGRUENT ORIGINS

The region is riddled with clashing backstories.
Some accounts detail a physical location, complete with maps composed in the styles of various earthly eras, the ledgers of lost ships,
diaries and daguerrotypes of assorted expeditions
on the brink of reckless abandon. Fierce heroic features.
Gazes that interrogate the interloper, piercing the sepia filth of antiquity.
Some accounts suggest a state of mind, or a state of grace,
a mostly metaphorical territory
that can only be accessed through secret doorways over distant hills and in cities.
Through fractures in space. Fissures in time.
The schizoid tropes of outsider art indicate the passage of mad afternoons and lost lifetimes.
The vanishings accumulate the more deeply you excavate these fractalizing timelines.
Rational enthusiasts of the zymoglyphic (insofar as reason will allow for such an enthusiasm)
often prefer the poetical assessment. It allows for more miracles.
Physics unbruised. Facts intact. Vast immaterial latitudes.
But where then do the travellers go who strike out in search of the shifting Source?
And where did all these fragments come from?
Is every paradise a lost paradise? has heaven exploded?
Does the godhead bleed its creeds across the sky in these witch-doctored photographs
while we contemplate the wreckage forensically?
Massive industrial projects have been engaged in the territory
On the heels of these ambiguous missions.
Do canny tycoons launder money through these wormholes?
The Zymoglyphic Society refuses to unpuzzle this issue definitively.
But it trades on the suggestion of a certainty with-held,
when the region clearly and in all accounts rises from the gnostic froth of the unknowable.

5. SECRET AUCTIONS

We are a disparate community, we Zymophiles and Zymopaths,
we who chase fugitive echoes of the unreal
through the nooks and crannies and clammy modern pauses of every encounter
through the alleys and arcades of every uneasy city.
Some of us emerged from obscene degrees of affluence
Some of us collaged our tattered maps of neverland in suburbs and hovels and factory towns.
The clubs in which we congregate run the bloody spectrum from treehouse to penthouse to cathouse
from houses of worship to dens of iniquity and miasmic mixes of the two.
As with most life-eating obsessions, our faith is a form of shopping.
We receive invitations through the poetry of consecutive highway billboards
and garbled newsflashes heard at random on broken radios, through neighboring windows.
We congregate in shady locations i am not at liberty to disclose, even in retrospect.
We compare degrees of damage. Jagged jigsaw bits of neverland.
A glove whose favorite hand was seen in a dream, attached to a bird-headed priestess.
Wind-up butterflies on piano-wire leashes that issue forth from a music box cocoon.
A telephone that connects you with the child you were when it's plugged into a bolus of earthworms.
An assortment of perfumed polaroids that have been used as a currency by a community of ghosts.
These are the troubling treasures we bring to these meetings.
Disfigured dissolute reprobates from every walk of life, selling our own organs and essences
for the keys to a quadrant of cloud cuckoo land that might maybe just maybe bring us closer to its core, to a version of the region that won't decompose into pixie dust at the first flush of relevance.
Zymoglyphic junkies, hustling for the crumbs of an ambiguous Elysium.

6. ISOMORPHIC PSYCHODRAMA #9

Something happened with us, that very first day,
our very first spin through the hall of dioramas
a naked allegory for you and me, reflecting our proclivities.
But it always happens, whenever crossed paths get fused by pheromones.
Mutual appetites are engaged and sacramentalized.
The big museum made of inside and outside provides little signs.
We know going in how good it will get at its best
and we know all the ways in which it will go wrong.
That Sunday, we could see it played out in fishtanks,
skeleton birds already mourning us
in the very moment of love's tremulous unfolding.
We took a tour of the chaos to come,
forensically prophetic puppet shows in sickly little terrariums.
What degenerate god-thing improvised the mess of us?
He feeds us when it suits him. On days like that day, he is tapping on
the glass.
the parts of our hearts that belong by nature to the Zymoglyphic region,
they felt the wreckage extending for miles of time and nonetheless said
yes to this.
In retrospect, our tryst was maybe born in its own crypt.
A vampire dance, acquiescing to every agony
for that first shattering gasp and the intermittent echo of communion.
The little windows that connect the scales are boarded up or invisible.
But a voodoo dollhouse needs my needles
and I will run them through a doll of me, half wanting it to work
because the broken me is gritty and believes things when they hurt.

7. SLEEK AND ANEMIC

If you've been reading the right magazines, you'll know
that in the zymoglyphic art world (such as it is),
the austerities of samurai chic have been streamlined into pure concept.
The process evokes an ambience of cultural contamination.
Fast food perfumes in a byzantine cathedral.
The prismatic primordial ooze cools and congeals to rust almost immediately,
raucous shamanic frenzy of the wayback and from thence into wonder
and then the gentle littleness of the Buddha brigade.
It's the nature of things, I suppose. Egregoric life cycles and such but now this.
Gallery culture. A prefab crème de la crème.
The jungles of the Zymoglyphic region will contrive hallucinations of your one real summer, just to keep you in their meshes.
Now they grow anemic art boutiques, staffed by mossy mannequins.
Reflecting the estrangement of the invader.
There's an element of parody in these hot plastic openings.
We were all in love with something in the age of wonder.
Now we have lots of ideas about love and lots of ideas about lots of ideas.
But the paintings get stranger the longer you look.
They seem to subtly and then flagrantly reflect your psychology and your struggles and your most meaningful personal symbols.
When was the last time you burst into tears in an art gallery?
By the time they catch you crying, the jungle owns you.
It recycles your collage meat into fictoplasmic reservoirs.
It's already growing new galleries,
customized to digest every facile flavor of hipness.
I'm in the woods, with the fungus lovers. Talking to the birds.
Melting everything I see into intoxicating thoughtstuff.
I left you some dream jelly. Let it get to know you.

8. MUSEUMS WITHIN MUSEUMS

There's a certain strain of nausea
that the psychetecture specialists like to cultivate.
Those whose task it is to preserve a gestalt of wonder
in the viscid gelatin of a constricted simulation.
Every home in Zymoglyphic City contains a detailed replica of itself
Temples contain little temples.
Museums contain little museums.
And, of course, the little museums contain littler museums.
The detailing is said to extend seven levels into the microcomuseum.
And presumably seven levels up into the macromuseum.
That's where the existential seasick elevator feeling comes from.
Gazing at a living doll of you and knowing that over your shoulder
In a direction that cannot be pointed to,
a slightly different you is gazing…and getting nauseous too.
The shadow of a bigger you, falling across the dollhouse of your life.
When we were children, we both dreamed a beach and strange playmates,
casting gigantic shadows on the sky.
Godlike, but oblivious.
Oblivious, but not yet afraid.

9. LET SLIP THE GRIP OF REASON

It won't help you here.
Despite the taxonomies and the scientific jargon,
Despite the bell jars and the specimen boxes and the lab coats of our technicians.
These are mere props and prompts and precautions.
Frames within which the wildlife runs riot.
Too measured a stance, too objective an attitude
could occlude our view of the miracles that matter.
The Zymoglyphic zone of experience,
(Whether it rages in the jungles and libraries and luxury hotels of the region itself or in little secret rooms like this)
is a state of mind and life and time
where/when objects dissolve into their evocations and associations,
where what we think we know about a thing has as much or more substance than the thing itself.
Matter yields to mind and this negligee you left behind
is filled by fifty ghosts of you and a thousand silky whispers,
The things they said to you, those others, as they peeled it from your shoulders.
Reason might determine that a rose is a rose.
But let the vestments fall away and this bleak autopsy
may bequeath a striptease.
A phoenix nest of burning bills that fuels your immanent annunciation.

10. ZYMOGLYPHIC DEMIMONDE

Oh, I've been to their parties.
The strangest rich people you've never seen,
like that infamous Rothschild surrealist masquerade,
but the mutations are real and more expensive than the moon.
Mannequins everywhere in these lush secret supper clubs.
Hovering Bellmer dolls and exquisite corpses.
House fungus confections on every menu.
All the gingerbread cottages growing creepy moss.
I've been addicted to drugs from other dimensions.
Shit you simply cannot get on the street.
The hosts indulge every passing pranasite, flaunting their collections,
Relics and inscrutable machines from a lost continent. Or is it an island?
Is it a wormhole orchard underworld? Is it a semi-sentient concept cluster?
Whatever it is or isn't, it's the baseline kink at these parties.
These pervy old monsters traffic in jagged fragments of Beyond.
Every travellers tale is worth something. Such baffling atrocities.
Gossip that would corrode all your paradigms.
That first party was a terror. I was young and hustling, then.
Beautiful and yours briefly for an arrogant but accurate fee.
Like an abduction experience. Out of my element.
Like I wasn't ready to run with a crew this bright, this clever, this deranged.
The spaces and the subtle graces between people eluded me.
We have this in common: nonstalgia. we ache for an imaginary place.
The Zymoglyphic Region has become the locus for all our disparate obsessions because it seems to be a kind of crossroads where many imaginary places intersect with an intensity that gives their infoplasm a slippery but supple substance.
All over the world, these secret museums and eternal floating soirees.
After the accident, sometimes stormed or shut down or rainbow bombed.
The galleries runneth over. All these hauntings.
Artists in various mediums and disciplines, describing their contact
With zymoglyphic energies. Zymoglyphic entities. Zymoglyphic eternities.
And yet, these etiquettes.

Social predation and hierarchy, even in this soup of figments.
Gradations of the phantasmatic. Taxonomies of the spirit world.
Scientists with the strangest specialties. Rumors of you. Your potential.
They are grooming you for a great expedition.
Your great adventure will have no value in the waking world,
Except insofar as you report back to us.
The society insists on relentless rhapsodic documentation.
Those attuned will feel the windows in your gibberish,
And the cold wind from nowhere that blows through them.

11. DREAM PURGE

They're stitching up every wormhole.
Something went wrong out there.
They're closing all the exits, burning all the wardrobes.
We all had our suspicions.
The whole Zymoglyphic community grew leathery and shrill in its paranoia.
Who in the upper echelons could be instigating all this?
What's the agenda, Brenda?
They're slaughtering semi-mythical beasts out there, in the haunted woods.
They pulled me into it, the ugly stuff, like they always do.
Ugly is sometimes my specialty.
The whole region is howling in pain. We are suppressing the territory.
The things we build here don't work outside, in the real world.
The world that seems less real to us the longer we spend in collage country.
The collage catching fire now, photographs shriveling,
all black and golden at the edges.
Our technologies are distorted in translation..
The house fungus helps. We are seizing all the supplies.
All the great Zymoglyphic curators have been hunted into alcoves.
They play their game in secret now.
These dioramas are machines that plant themselves in your dreams.
We're chasing shadows through burning doorways, now.
They can smell it on you, the perfume of Otherness.
The stench of the Zymoglyphic.
Notes of civet and cinnamon to cloak a creeping cosmic sadness.
Common scents consumed at last by a cloud of olfactory madness.

12. CLOSING EVERY WORMHOLE

Every halfway haunted house.
Every impossible cabinet.
Every forbidden living book.
The conjunction of certain objects and influences can induce a wormhole situation.
Special teams are moving in.
Those churning holes in summertime clouds through which we have accessed and milked the hills of neverland.
You must hide all signs of your traffic with the ghost folk.
People are vanishing every day, their datatrails imploding, their place in our memories bleeding into a blur.
An astral disaster has necessitated a containment scenario.
We'll be getting back to real life, now.
Folding all this splendor into terms the realist can understand.
Racing through my own memories, seeking the spots on the surface of spacetime
where I experienced the deepest Otherness.
Cutting up those moments and hiding the fragments so they can't redact me
When the purge begins.
All those spots were bruised already by the slice of me that belongs to Them.
Drained of that Zymoglyphic essence.
All the old territories, decomposing into evidence.
The physics of my futurepast, getting tighter and tighter,
and yet more and more random.
The chance of a miracle getting slimmer and slimmer as the probabilities constrict.
We who still practice the precepts (despite the constrictions),
we meet in secret, sometimes in code.
Surrounded by shards of the great twisted mirror
that was the Zymoglyphic experience.
Rituals in the funhouse fragments of our last shattered paradise.

13. IT ALL WENT WRONG, SOMEHOW

Such bright beatific futures. Such luscious blue tomorrows.
All the fortunes we will make. All the grand adventures.
Sudden access to those unknown pleasures
afforded only to the outrageously privileged.
Then news of a disaster.
Its nature is ambiguous.
But everything is different now.
Something went wrong, somehow.
Crackling incoherent newsflashes from a war zone.
It's been distorted into art by the time it reaches us.
Vacation snaps ooze into brutal cartoons.
All her letters to the big back home read more and more like poetry.
What a ravishing disintegration.
The many worlds were smeared before us.
Ours for the feasting. Ours for the taking. Eternity on toast.
Did someone get too greedy?
Was this the region's design, all along?
To lure us into a place where our sweetest human dreams can unfold,
flourish and succumb to corruption in the space of an evening?
Just so the territory can taste the fever of a dream that is dying.
I bump into people who worked with me, at that first excavation.
I marvel at their ruined faces, then remember my own.
I sympathize with the ravaged region, not so much with my fellow victims.
My taste, and therefore my doom, has always bled towards the decadent.
The boldest, most heroic golden dreams,
spoiling into obsessive, silvery horror.

14. DJ HOUSE FUNGUS

When the exploitation begins in earnest,
they start moving in the worker bees.
The drones and the gnomes and their wild children,
going native so quickly.
A sound from the collective oneiric underground,
something that throbs so close to the source of things
The source of thought and feeling.
They made slums here, housing for the slaves in all but name.
But the jungle always intrudes with its psychoactive moss and its lily dust.
The jungle is always hungry.
A sound coming up from the dewslick sidestreets.
All by itself it's like the scritching and scratching
of something verminous and electric at the back of the brain.
Under the influence of the house fungus,
these mutant bric-a-brac mushrooms,
whole vistas of experience unfold in every beat.
You see your moments preserved in a sonic jelly, an invisible museum.
You feel the expansion of infinite museums within the sprawling opera.
"I am your broken robot. I am your howling moondog. Go with me to the movies."
Raves in rough cathedrals the jungle improvised to eat our prayers.
A crazed kid gets ghostly and hears things we can't
until he makes the noise with his machines.
Prismatic vinyl smuggled into foreign territories.
The Zymoglyphic region blooms in every room where his students spin.
He has schooled them in the language of the scissorbirds.
He has shown them where the glamorous glue resides
and how to coax it into explosions.
On the dancefloor. Or wherever.
A generation of Zymodelic half-breeds were conceived
to his sinister symphony.
Infection Vectors of a HyperVirus.
(epidemics 1, 2, and 3).

15. ZYMOGLYPHIC NIGHTLIFE

You can only get there by boat, maybe.
Or I'm flying in and the clouds are so exotic here, swollen with figments.
Here from parts unknown and parts known all too well.
Here to indulge in some adult entertainments.
The flashing nightclubs, the kids all wigged on house fungus.
I'm wearing a gas mask like all the tourists, to protect me from the fumes.
There are boughs of densely populated skeleton trees hanging heavy with alien fruit. But I am not a scientist. I came here for pleasure.
Since last summer. Since the accident. I am living for pleasure.
If you take off the gasmask and breathe this place, you will never want to leave.
And many never do. So many sensualists go missing here.
The angel arcades. The sacred cinema. The interspecies sex club menageries.
The ectosexual ghost bordellos. They grow a room to meet your needs.
Everything you've ever wanted. Only moreso.
Famished from a hell of the flesh, there are meaty murders on the menu.
A row of glittering restaurants.
No language, no ethnicity, and no cuisine you can definitively identify.
Something maddening and unsatisfying about the zymoglyphic expedition.
It always feels like a dream.
When you're ready to accept the region's teachings,
the mask comes off and the dreaming never ends again, if it ever did.
But tonight I am averting my gaze from burning bushes.
I am hiding from the signs. I am evading all epiphanies.
I am keeping it shallow and craven and depraved. Oh, the glamor of it all.
We cross paths at some point, you and I.
Strangers still, but with a rattle of deja voodoo.
Then the orgy upgrades into a labyrinthine epic of erotic pursuit.
Like all the love songs and the hunting songs.
We are shifting shapes as we chase each other, each of us playing the prey at times,
Each of us hunting.
In flight, I grab your ankle and we hover over a great expanse of black

ocean.
I promise to fuck you desperately on the baccarat tables
of elegant continental casinos.
I promise to hook you on drugs unknown to mainstream science.
Look at all these businessmen, gone mad from too much pleasure.
The reports they're sending back to the home office
must sound like the ravings of rabid bonobos.
You always want me to take the mask off, but it's my only defense
against you.
Without this mask, I'd marry your carnival.
Your snakedancers, your freakshows and peepshows.
I've been looking for that pink room in the 3rd floor window all my life.
Seen from the street when all was lost and hopeless.
But every time, at the threshold, I remember, it's the longing that I love.
To achieve the room is to lose it, says my cunning or my cowardice.

16. DEGRADATION OF THE TERRITORY

When we first started developing the region,
it had this filigreed victorian splendor.
Steam-powered simulations of its last colonization,
Running still to put us at ease, perhaps.
All this voluptuous clip art in crisis. All these feral collage chimeras
and disquieting juxtapositions.
But the Zymoglyphic Region ultimately reflects the character
(and compulsions) of the beholder.
So many greedy bastards slithered in, heads full of junk.
The zone was so accommodating, at first, but it turned on us.
To protect itself. Now it reflects only our madness.
A terrifying decomposition of visions and values creeps in.
Structural and psychological disintegration. Mutating memories.
All the important people losing their minds in the perfumed mist.
The faerie-tech nanoswarms we've been breathing.
Since she said what she said. Since I did what I did.
They say there was some disaster. Only one disaster? Only one?
That crash was just the climax.
There's been this eerie creeping and crumbling between us,
en route to this fantastic catastrophe.
There's the baying of hounds, but we grow wings when the fear sets in.
Like vultures or like sphinxes, depending on our mood.
The magicks have congealed here.
Everything between us is lit up with static flashes,
recut in our heads for maximum hysteria.
Ancient monuments and mysteries desecrating themselves
to fill the air with shame.
On the fungus, we can see this modular corporate disease
chewing its way through the etiquettes of genteel Zymoglyphic society.
We didn't understand the way the biota works
before we offered up our fates to the ineffable mechanics of its digestion.
A violent edge has emerged in all of our transactions.
The ambient paranoia has a kick and a music all its own.
We are crossing over into a wounded twilight,
the cosmos as defunct shopping center. Endless and obscene.
The logos proliferating. Mythologies pimped by technicians.
Our god buttons pushed by everything we see until the best thing in us
Is ruddy and raw and chafed from abusive invocations.

17. CHASING TRACES OF IMPOSSIBLE PLACES

We've been everywhere, you and I, and everywhere is dull.
We've seen the seven wonders they talk about and the seven hundred others.
Sobbing again in some hotel room. Again, that Caesar feeling.
Or that napoleon and josephine feeling. Or alexander and his horse.
No new worlds to conquer. The grail has been drained of every drop
Of its silver liquid light.
This metaphysical wanderlust drew the wreck of us together.
We would taste the ten million pains and pleasures.
Bold, intrepid travellers.
Certain that there are little windows into eternity hidden everywhere.
Were we so special, or do Zymoglyphic types everywhere form little
ghost gangs and chaos covens and forbidden book circles in their spooky teens?
We're comparing the maps that we made privately,
sometimes with crayons or with blood in a state of reckless exorcism.
For reasons that will become obvious, the sponge is sacred to us.
The pores and perforations suggest worlds within worlds.
We'd visit all the galleries, all the flea markets, all the abandoned houses,
our secret senses tingling, casting the meshes of perception,
searching every object for residual hints of Otherness.
Some exhibits shred the membrane more overtly than others.
We'd run into each other, lovers of the Zymoglyphic vibration.
In various disguises. In various lives.
Meeting again and again in the most unlikely places.
A few of us vanished back into the flux and muddle of social life and time.
A healthy choice, if health is what you're into.
And yet once the Zymoglyphic region has touched you through its artifacts
or its mere ambience, there's no going back to the game of cages.
What heartbreak for one never so scarred to marry one of these monsters!
We settle into a parody of domestic life, partly just to numb the hunger,
But we are devils in boxes, incubating mischief.
The call of Beyond rises up in us again.
The Zymoglyphic Region is a crossroads place.
It barely frames a million rabbit holes into everywhen.

We who are its acolytes and its paladins, we will always be led away.
No ghost of home can hold us,
for we have known the rough mercury magic of the road.
The night road. The winged dust.
Receiving real indications of other worlds moving through us.
My attention peels you to a core that you live for,
but the core of me is always elsewhere.
Or so I tell myself as I service you fanatically
And live on your moon-milk like a feral ghost baby.

18. HOME OF ALL HEARTS OR HONEYTRAP?

The Zymoglyphic region will be what you want it to be.
It will provide you with puzzles and trials.
It will unsolve all your problems.
The heroic journeys grow on world trees here.
When they ripen and hit the pavement, their meat emits a stink
only a swarm of flies could love.
Out here on the frontier of what is possible.
The desires of every traveller, reflected in the landscape.
Some early explorers thought they'd found a kind of heaven.
I guess we always do, the first time.
But it always goes sour somehow. Even when it doesn't.
Even when you miss all the glitches, it feels so good just to breathe,
and you start to wonder if the region grew all this to bewitch you.
It will grow the kind of people you want to be with.
A very pragmatic intelligence at work amongst the tulpas.
We thought we could harness the force that drives all these shifting
shapes.
But there's a fresh strain of strangeness emerging in the latest harvest.
Something altogether alien and vaguely malevolent,
with no reassuring sheen of junkshop wizardry.
The soupcan babies spell out difficult truths with little noodles.
"It eat you". The region is obviously digesting us. First the dreams.
Then the rest of us. Images recur like clumsy motifs in our wildest
hallucinations.
This place is trying to tell us something. The soup says "get out".
We interpret the message endlessly, as we approach the place of
dissolution.
We were all seeing slightly different versions, the overlap almost artistic.
It disguises itself as wherever you want to be.
And sometimes it knows you better than you do,
and you don't know where heaven is until it shows you.
And then it eats you. Then it eats you. Then it eats you.
I'm soothing myself successfully by kissing every tree that grows your
facsimile.
Seeing you everywhere as I starve to death,
as I wither from the lack of something fundamental.
Something that looks like you when the region reads my mind.
No place safe to sit, in these waning hours. Every surface is alive here.

Alive and hungry. Every car. Every building. Every museum.
Especially the museums. I'm inside Her now. Inside Her Absolute.
I'm naming Her after you. Before She unmakes me.
My spurned salvation. My ravenous paradise.
Do I taste like fire? Or like the bomb that brings it?

19. THE HUNGRY JUNGLE

Some suspect that this entire cluster of islands
might be the remains of some crashed angelic entity.
They say its soft technology is still at work beneath the skin of things.
We have been reading the mind of an angel.
Its memory banks disclose infinitudes.
It grows people in jellybags, just to hold all the impossible memories.
It expresses itself in lifeforms, in reckless fecundity.
All these beings that bloom within its synchro-mesh,
some of whom are wired to imagine that they are individuals,
making choices of their own.
The natives decompose into a cloud of sickly synaesthesia
when you try to bring them back to snivelization.
You can't bring this collage girl home to mother.
But we went in deep, she and I, discovering and documenting
each bouquet of aberrations.
Some of our visions were ineffably alien.
Some of them all too familiar.
Who can say what actually, factually unfolded here?
The ambient gases make us all mad.
The clockwork cicadas and the birds of prey. A malevolent environment.
Unknowable lifeforms that bloom outside our archetypes.
Underneath their faceplates, the soft circuitry.
The churning wormholes.
The tendrils that slap and slither behind all the paintings.
How many expeditions have gone missing?
So many children go running from the camp to go walkabout
With the aborigine kidlings.
The landscape goes mad. We are oozing through the mist.
I maintain a little house on the outskirts.
Beyond this point, the physics get soft. Mushy. Mutable.
The jungle hungers for thee, my love.
Oh, how the jungle hungers for your flavor.

20. A MUSEUM OF US

Traveling for a long time. On a mission of some kind.
So many quarrels and reconciliations.
Finding each other and losing each other ten million times.
Shifting from shape to shape.
Finally letting go, finally going off in our own direction.
But we are led by figment and subtertfuge to a huge museum of us,
a haunted place where the tableaux and dioramas
Illustrate moments of our love affair through the lens of allegory and fever dream.
We are flashing. Blinking here. All the old photographs.
The missing girl kits catching fire. We are on a river, floating into the dark.
The statues. The maps. The baubles under glass.
Models of our sacred locations.
Abstract diagrams of our most significant positions.
Costumes we wore in our lovegames, on our famous dates..
Serious performers reading aloud from our loveletters in sprawling ceremonies.
Intergalactic ritual tributes, conducted at the nexus of many worlds.
Future generations pouring through the doorways. Loving us. Quoting us.
Also, the dark times. Our combat staged as modern dance kung fu.
Possible futures. The two of us getting old together, despite the vicissitudes. Or not.
Branching out into other museums. From some vantage points,
In some futures, the palace of us looks small and sad.

21. THEIR LANGUAGE IS ALIVE

It's such a funny, seductive patois.
The English they seem to speak in the zymoglyphic region.
A musical mash-up of several twilight tongues.
It sounds utterly alien when you first hear it,
but all the fungal excretions and perfumed gases affect the language centers,
Exposing us to a viral intelligence which bonds with the parts of us that speak.
Their language is ALIVE.
Trashy things we say come out as poetry. All our thoughts get stranger on contact.
No statement is left well enough alone. The Zymoglyphic Syntax slithers within us..
Hearing an argument through the floorboards,
it sounds like angels or oceans clashing.
To learn a few words, it changes you.
Keep your tourist gasmask on, and it just sounds like the night
is always alive with gibberish.
But the names for things change the thing that is named.
Secret academies. Adepts in the art and science of the hologrammar.
Angelspeak. Speaking in the raw,
half-teleplasmic dialect of the ghost folk,
it's changing the structure of our faces.
The Logos grows tattoos on the surfaces of our auric eggs.
Fierce new glyphs with their own agendas.
Listen closely to the bubbling behind the slang.
You will hear sinister structures emerging in it.
We will speak in emotional aggregates.
Try not to listen to the words they use to speak you into being.
Not every character is made for metatext.
This language you're speaking, it was once a lifeform.
It is decomposing into a plague of glyphs and incantations.
A programming language from another dimension.
Delirious study often yields the cheat codes.
When you say these shadow things sideways, mutations ensue.
It's why we came here, after all.

22. DESPERATE SIGNAL/SECRET LOVER

I would never have gone back if I didn't get your message.
Things went so sideways before that perfect final day and then goodbye.
I left you to melt back into the strangeness and charm of the old hotel and the protean hellscape that churned always outside its frilly windows.
You seemed so happy there, seeing yourself in the chaos, maybe.
I'd already awakened you from one dream too many.
I saw hovering signs and fluttering omens for days before your package arrived.
One of those quintessentially zymoglyphic moments,
when you're surprised at how unsurprised you are.
Your letter sounded just like that. Like someone melting.
The way you'd get in the hotel when all the reasonable people went away.
Like every element of design in your environment was some kind of puzzle.
A puzzle that unpuzzles you as you solve it.
Then you're a deconstructed school of moments loose in a soup of delirium.
I've built a new life back here, in the world that thinks it's real.
My wife can't know about us, what we were to each other.
She can't know I ever went that deep with someone, that cold and complete.
No one can know what happened in collage country
Where love is never linear and scissorbirds sing angels into being.
Sometimes I daydreamed that you would follow me here,
determined to take some kind of revenge and ruin my ordinary life.
But you left that to me.
You knew something in me would stay with you.
Something missing in me always.
They all come running, the men and women you bewitched.
We compared letters and wounds and memories of you in the hunting lodge,
out at the perimeter.
We would all walk into that thresher again.
Did someone trick us all here to kill all his rivals and posses you completely?
No one who knew you well enough to fall victim would be so naïve.

You are not the kind of person who can be possessed.
By gods or men or anything.
Mythologies get slaughtered in your crisis after crisis.
Your beauty is bigger than the concept of god. You possess us instead.
In my luckiest mirror, I can feel you smile inside me.

23. AFTER THE ACCIDENT

Same old story,
since way before Babylon.
Malevolent interlopers try to harness
the savage energies
of the collective unconscious.
People beyond the reach of blame
or regret.
The jungle
tried to regrow its architecture,
even as the blast ripped through it.
All these sudden ruins of the great society.
Officers and technicians
from dubious institutions,
Taking readings
and assessing the damage.
Ambulance fleets and hovering hospitals.
We treat those who were born here
with special bandages.
Mythic territories have been brutalized into fact
by the blunt atomic impact.
All the living buildings
just massive corpses now.
A howling wind whipping
through the chime-afflicted trees.
The ghosts of those scrambled by the great disaster.
They'll be dragging the lake for centuries,
fresh dead in every mesh.
This is what it was like to love you.
A festival season,
then a rupture from nowhere.
Then you became the nowhere.
My obsession shades slowly
from the chill of religion
to the fanatically forensic.
We never know what hit us,
Or what hit who we were
before getting broken.
Before the breaking, we were all the same person

24. RAINBOW BOMB

We're figuring out how to weaponize the Dreaming.
We assembled fugitive scientists from various broken nations
that flew too close to the black sun of empire.
Smuggling artifacts and organisms from inside the Region.
Set it off in the desert, they said. What could go wrong, they said.
The paradise that ensues flourishes and dies in the space of a day.
Grainy black and white documents of our hideous experiments.
We watch them when we've all been awake too long,
like stag films. We were too far gone again.
Only the scream of a stranger could clue us in to a twisted taboo.
Take a job like this, you leave your moral compass at the door.
When you get released, you can reclaim it as a joke.
And wear it as a nostalgic affectation.
But it's not something that ever grows back. Not really.
Doctors in goggles and black rubber gloves.
The things they do with missing children these days.
The things they allow. The things we get away with.
There ought to be a law.
We can't confirm a negative result.
This bomb might be the best thing that ever happened to some
territories.
What if you turn some inconvenient rogue state into wonderland by
mistake?
It's egg-shaped and it hovers there in the shed, bleeding panic.
We are evacuating all the seaside resorts and pleasure centers.
"Evacuate my pleasure centers," said the actress to the bishop.
All the carnivals are creaking and sobbing in the dusk,
the animals mangy and uncaged.
I've seen the team that dropped the first one.
In the bright spirit of their great adventure
and in their gibbering institution epilogues.
We tried to pick men with no families at first.
Then, typically, R & D forgot to give a fuck.
The families fare no better than the bombers.
It spreads, somehow, the half-life.
Drop this thing on a city,
watch all the billboards and screens and magazines come to uneasy life.
A rainbow grenade can bring an advert into skin,

But you can't control the flow of its commerce.
She runs wild for as long as she can,
then slows down and twitches and molts at the first touch of realism.
I'm holed up here, watching the streets,
Watching the models molt, waiting for a signal.
Waiting for a sign that I'll be gone before I ever crave penance.
A sign that the razorlaced rainbows are coming
and the tedium of my timespace is grinding to a convenient climax.

25. I WOULD DO IT WRONG AGAIN

Something broke in me out there.
In retrospect, I can see the signs and the omens and the recurring motifs.
I can see the burning bushes.
I can see myself running naked at breakneck speed
into wheat thresher after wheat thresher.
My body a red cloud of sudden chum.
I can't tell how much of this clarity is illumination
and how much is just sheer mathematical perspective.
Or if there's a difference.
But the scissorbirds are circling and hissing your secret names.
And you need to know that I would do it wrong again.
We were lost in the funhouse from the start, I think.
Chasing distorted reflections through a series of looking glass bedrooms,
seizing your thread and unmazing myself
to find that the world was always just a mess of shattered mirrors.
Broken glass and a lost feeling and disembodied angry vibrations.
But there is a love in this blighted place,
and I needed to be this broken to know it.
So even as I burn your villages and commodify your mysteries
I am thanking you. Always thanking you.
And I'm letting go of harsh thoughts about you.
Whatever you were doing here, I was doing it too.
The altered boy in me only learns from his wounds.
So I endeavor to shake the all too alluring ambience of tragedy.
And more authentically attune myselves to your frequency of eternity.
We took photos of our molten core of intimacy.
The lens got scratched. We won't ever be friends.
But the voices that were freed in me,
as I pantomimed your worship of the automatic,
the voices serve me well and what I lost in you is still mine to spend.
If I don't see you in the everywhen,
know this, my possessed pretend friend,
I would do it all
I would do it wrong again.

26. THE DARKEST CONTINENT

We thought we'd seen everything, mapped everyplace
in our fever for exploitation did I say exploitation?
I meant exploration. We always mean to say exploration.
Every tycoon weeping like Caesar,
sad that there are no more undiscovered worlds to plunder.
A sense of grinding science and oneiric poverty crept
into every quadrant of our privilege.
"but then...the Zymoglyphic Region!"
A poster in the waiting room of a seedy travel agency.
For one shining moment, hidden in the hustle and hush of history,
you could book a vacation or pursue a vocation
in the thriving colonization
of neverland.
Every time we discover the Region, we go in with naked hearts
and eyes all spun from the wonder.
Then we remember the monsters we were
before the pungent fungal perfumes made us children again.
We grow up again and impose our agendas
On the last lost continent. The place that eats us when we dream.
It complies with our projections.
It reflects them...improves them, even...to better facilitate our
dissolution.
It all goes wrong. Every time. "discovery".
Exploration...exploitation...annihilation.
An annihilation so complete
that the happenings are erased from our histories,
leaving a residue of cryptic clues
to be sniffed out and followed obsessively
by another plague of juicy would-be predators
who live a tacky dream of will and agency.
But who are possessed by a hunger
that craves its own extinction.

27. A SUMMER IN EVERY KISS

The experience of falling in love in the Zymoglyphic region
or under Zymoglyphic circumstances
Is arguably the deepest and most complex aesthetic experience
that can be had in this life.
No one woos like a surrealist.
Other strategies might be warmer or more humane,
but the fetishistic intensity, the savage humor, and the symbolic density
can't really be touched by any other seduction style.
All who are kissed on the brain by mad love have tasted the
Zymoglyphic, of course,
when the moon looms too too closely.
when all the songs contain backmasked witches, hissing your name.
When the TV speaks urgently in glossy parables
and emergent faces in the wallpaper daisies
scream "love the Other. Love the Other."
in shrill violinsect voices.
Time gets soft for Zymoglyphic lovers.
And time at the best of times is fraying at the edges.
And the emotional content of several lifetimes
can be compressed
into the timespace of a weekend or an evening…or a kiss.
But no one can stay there, so we need to bring back treasures.
Objects and moments encoded with meaning that will open up inside us
When we say the magic word.
The feral teenage summer
and its endless empty promises
the necessity and the futility
and the swoon of future nostalgia
and childhood prophecy
alive in the Now.
The wet life and the chapped death of it.
We kiss again.

28. I TOOK OFF MY GASMASK

Before entering the territory, we received some instruction.
Common sense safety strategies for survival in the kingdoms of the unreal.
Oblique films on super 8.
Detailing the dangers of operating obsolete machines with inscrutable functions.
Narrated in a language none of us could identify.
Subtitles like crack-head haiku.
But we were made to watch them,
as if some moral lesson was implicit in the films and subliminally infectious.
Burn victims. Glowing green bandages.
Surrealist crime scenes and industrial accidents.
Murders so sexy they melt the projector.
The film I'm in jumps and crackles and shrivels in the gate.
But the gasmask is obvious. The gasmask is irrefutable.
The gasmask is key to the whole operation.
The Zymoglyphic Region is alive at all times
with swarming psychoactive spores of various types.
So many conflicting trips in collision,
agreed to every time you breathe.
So there were more and more outsiders,
more and more immigrants and speculators and entrepreneurs.
And customized designer gasmasks were the rage
Often in a filigreed faux victorian design (fungal punk, if you will)
That conjured the romance of empire
even as you stagger through its excrement.
The gasmask keeps us from "going native",
from melting into this place.
But she wanted to see my face.
She wanted to see my face.
She wanted to see my face.

29. FEED ME TO THE SPIDER QUEEN

At some point in the sometimes tedious, sometimes turbulent corporate colonization process,
the Society started referring to the aboriginal Zymoglyphicans as "ghost folk",
evoking the tendency of the natives to seemingly flicker in and out
of material existence
the way some martyrs rise again and again
to experience all the shades and gradations of murder.
The natives themselves mutate and shift shapes
to meet our unspoken expectations.
They at times seem to embody and enforce the intentions
Of the region itself, like tools it grew to study us.
You could spend several scholarly lifetimes surfing
The fractalizing cosmologies of their philosophy.
Agents of the Zymoglyphic Society have compiled
A vast library of recordings.
Alien fruit plucked from the angel-heavy boughs
of that haunted orchard where the living lovesongs grow.
After our third assignation,
when the flavor of our fever changed so decisively,
I exited the hotel to face a ghost boy in the street,
deftly playing a strange guitar with three necks and too many strings,
singing FEED ME TO THE SPIDER QUEEN.
A ghostly folksong from a time of fanatical human sacrifice.
A pretty kid in the slums couldn't hope for much
but to be Meat for Her,
she who spins the webs of time in which we are enmeshed
as we quaintly dream duration.
If she drools for thee in dreams, you see a specialist for three weeks.
The hard knock world becomes your orgy.
You are a superstar, of a sort.
Then she eats you.
Then she eats you.
Then she eats you.
And you find in the mess she makes that the fun is just beginning.
A violinsect lands on my forehead.
I give the kid some poignant polaroids
and I go back to pondering the shape of our relationship.

30. THE SOCIETY IN SHAMBLES

After the massive unmentionable disasters
that shattered our maps and cast our affairs in disarray,
the Societus Zymoglyphicus
was a hot dreamy mess for a good long while.
It began with such heroic dignity, our golden age,
bold explorers tinted with a shimmer of already dubious innocence.
Gorgeous myth-sick uberscum, standing fearlessly at the rim of the unknowable.
But the serpent slipped in with us when we occupied the long lost garden.
And now portraits of the robber barons whose legacies we have corrupted
leer in judgement in our fancy clubs
while we count all the ways we don't give a fuck.
The Society's collection of Zymoglyphic artifacts
has been dispersed and hidden in secret museums,
where emergency wormholes into the undermind of man are under construction.
The fraying of physics? Already in progress.
No more laws of nature. Just loose general guidelines.
Then the schisms and the gangwars,
then the espionage and the purges.
And now we conduct our affairs in catacombs,
weaving together the shreds of our faithless faith,
Chanting a great revival into being.
Not a resurrection. A reconciliation
of principles that have gone unmingled
for one too many forevers.

31. BUGHOUSE PHILOSOPHY

Now that all our search parties have gone missing,
now that our impossible comic book technologies
have surrendered their candy logics to the encroachments of realism,
now that our elegant maps have abstracted themselves
into a continuum of massacres,
our only way through, our only way home
resides in the fragmented casualties.
The same obsessive explorers who thrilled us
with their implausible case histories,
their psychedelic showdowns in malevolent tulpa gardens,
mercury lie-traps that improvise lifeforms to bewitch and consume the seeking eye.
Refugees from a foetid breeding bank
of increasingly unearthly delights.
We went to see patient zero in the bughouse.
A lush magic mountain of a bughouse,
catering to the most exotic moths and the jeweled cocoons
of well-connected caterpillars.
Soothing sounds and fragrances.
Sharp corners and sleek surfaces.
No patterns for his boggled mind to play with.
Surrounded by stenographers at all times,
taking down the fractured testament of an extravagantly human mind,
a cloud-sculpting glass cathedral of a mind,
that flew too close to the quasar-spitting invisible anti-sun
of Mind itself.
An emergent intelligence that dwarfs and generates and supersedes the human.
The room gets cold like math is cold.
The radio chops up those Goldberg variations
with jagged slabs of black static.
The patient assumes a cracked facsimile of lucidity
and seems to glow as he describes
his inherently heretical philosophy…

32. HOW MANY MADE IT BACK?

"A great voice.
and then a great movement of voices,
moving across the face of the silence…"
In the wake of every great launching,
another ship or plane or séance,
bound for strange tides under too many moons,
in the weeks after we would wait for news.
Often a pause.
Then the telegrams getting stranger and stranger.
Phrases that make you a little bit dizzy
and you sit down suddenly
like you need to digest them.
Origami lilies of meaning unfolding in the aquarium of memory.
If you do a little digging, you'll find that no one made it back.
We've lost several expeditions down there.
They lose their minds and slough all connections to the homeworld.
Values. Family. Programming. Backstory.
All irrelevant in the Zymoglyphic mist.
Consumed by more primordial attractions.
You might see people wearing their faces if you go looking.
Behind the face, just the junkyard and the jungle
and the eerie ways in which we are all the same.
Sometimes someone makes it halfway back,
like Squamata's one-man symposium of gibberish.
Or like me, I suppose,
real again but so deeply haunted
that my shadows multiply and whisper invitations
At every midnight crossroads.

33. REPORTING BACK TO THEE

The papers will say that you seduced me.
That you coerced me into meat for your crusade.
But my brain consented to the washing.
My small self, a petty tyrant, willing to be dethroned.
Receiving orders always comes as a great comfort.
I know you barely know me.
Maybe because you're the last person I spoke to
before I took on this assignment,
you have come to represent
a more innocent
conception of reality
and its relationship with consciousness.
A way of seeing that I miss very much,
Despite the grandeur of my more recent delusions.
But I do like to think about you censoring my reports,
taking out the parts that might save me.
Redacting my rescue indefinitely.
So deep undercover, I'm of nine minds about most things.
At the core of us, an oscillating tone.
A transmigrational frequency,
the shriek that calls me home.
As I am folded into myth,
as I explode into collage,
as I go to pretty pieces in a labyrinth
of disfigured refractions
and sub-personalities
and parallel selves,
still my objective burns like a diamond of the mind,
at the core of all this thought and sensation.
My narrations are increasingly unreliable
as the Zymoglyphic BiotaMorph applies its surgeries to my echo,
but your smile was always dreamy pure America to me.
Dead or alive, in the light of your lies,
I'm reporting back to Thee.

Part II:
Cantos 34-66

34. REMAINS OF A ZYMONAUT

One of the most prized pieces in the Zymoglyphic Museum's collection
is this trunk of fragments, purchased at a secret auction,
after existing purely in the realm of rumor for decades.
Allegedly, this assortment of expositions, speculations, and reminiscences
constitute the memoir of a secret agent of some kind sent undercover
to divine the hidden agendas of the Zymoglyphic Enterprise.
Other accounts suggest that this "Jason Squamata"
may have been a field agent for the House of Mercury
Or one of the more obscure Advertising Dynasties.
He may have been embroiled in some fungus-dusted strain of industrial espionage.
Who he was working for may remain ambiguous.
But he was scribbling these reports on cocktail napkins,
in moss-eaten journals, on Hotel Zymoglyphic stationery.
His mission apparently became complicated by his involvement
with an ostensibly civilized ghost girl who was raised in the region.
The details and parameters and trajectory of their relationship,
like Squamata's objective, must remain…ambiguous,
but the whole erotic psychodrama is alive between the lines
in the relationship between these disparate fragments.
To sift through these undated, apparently random musings
on the nature of life and time in the Zymoglyphic Region
is to become immersed in the disintegration of a crafty modern mind.
We participate in its melting as the starlost seeker's Voice gets louder in our heads.
The ultimate denouement of this spiraling sequence of fever dreams
from profane to sacred and back again plays out in the bodymind of the beholder.
It doesn't matter what happened to Squamata.
He was only ever a voice your dream grew
to tell you magic words that you already knew.
Sessions of contact with the trunk and its contents can be arranged.
For the serious collector. By appointment only.
The Museum has been good enough to provide the casual Zymophile
with these transcriptions.
Some critics have suggested that the author was mentally ill
and tragically inveigled into the Zymoglyphic lifestyle (which exalts the

unsane).
Whichever order the fragments are presented in, they paint a portrait
of an exotic consciousness in pursuit of its own oblivion,
inherently puerile but equating the highest rapture with the sloughing of
self.
Other critics aren't even sure there is a trunk of documents,
much less a Squamata. One of the problems of practicing magic
in an age of rabid reason
is that the real gooey voodoo of it is all jungled up
with the cloaks and tuxedoes and tricky showbiz shadow cabinets.
To be an utterly modern person, to be truly Zymoglyphic,
is to cultivate multiple origin stories. And lock them in a trunk.

35. HAUNTED BY THE GHOST OF ALL THAT ISN'T

When you remove the mask, the densely populated silence
goes to work on you immediately.
You breathe the perfumes
and the gases
and the pheromonal spore-storms
that distort the perceptions
of all whose faces go naked here.
Sophisticated nanoswarms
in faerie queen drag
are storming through your pores,
weaving fresh meshes
of synapse and sensation.
Every public space
becomes a garden of forking paths.
And we can see the sum totaled bolus
of all the paths not taken,
awake and coiling in the same space,
every choice exploding into specters.
Our heads were messy from all the antic raving.
All the forks and high roads
that our affair could have taken.
All the truths too freely spoken
and the pretty lies withheld.
All the lovers we could have been,
all the better and more broken me's
and missing you's and different you's
and there's an Us in every window.
The night you went out naked
under that deliciously unforgivable koalaskin coat.
Now your naked echoes scar the arcade,
like a doodle by Delvaux.
All the better men I could have been for you.
So many lives where we ended up together after all.
Surely more than with the average situation.
And also spastic sketches of trauma wherein we are made
from stabbing lines of rage.
We are learning to burn, despite the nebula.
The perfumed garden where stars are born.

36. SENTIENT LIQUID

Were there mermaids in the Zymoglyphic Region
before they saw the concept of the mermaid in our minds?
The documents that survive from the earliest expeditions
describe a thickening of the ocean
as the S.S. Interloper approached the first island,
becoming almost gelatinous once they were close enough
to disembark and reach the beach.
One scurvy-scorched seaman insists
that faces were forming in the oceanic muck.
Beautiful women and men who rose with the waves as if to kiss him.
They have fish tails in his memory
because the mind tends to mash up experience and expectation
so recklessly
that it's a wonder we see anything but our preconceived notions.
Or perhaps they were transitioning from reflecting the essence of marine life
To reflecting the essence of man. God help them. God help us all.
These sentient liquid lifeforms are loose in the plumbing of the Capital City,
Splashing from our faucets, growing throats to scream with
a shrill gurgle you'll never want to hear again.
Intermingled liquid lads and lassies sick from all the poisons.
Or diluted into misshapen insensibility,
murmuring idiot epics of a bizarro atlantis.
In luxury hotels like this one, the fluids they sluice through
are purified.
The tap calls forth a much friendlier and more interesting
kind of lifeform.
That's right, lovers, get wet in our deluxe
"enchantment under the sea" honeymoon suite.
Fill your heart-shaped Jacuzzi with a gelatinous harem
of shapeshifting nymphs and nixies.
Consummate the communion of Venusian oyster and trident of Poseidon
(or pearl to pearl, conch to conch)
in a lascivious bubblebath made of sleazy sentient liquid.
You haven't lived until you've seen your seed rise
from the freshly baptized torso of that special someone

as a steaming school of fish babies.
In a more innocent, less profitable age, the siren only had a song to
charm us with.
Now there's all this greedy moisture.
And the craven, abusive appetites of the ugly American.
In the lobby, they sell lockets that each contain
an imprisoned globule of intelligence.
If you don't show up, I'll send you one and he'll ask you where it came
from.
Never noticing the way it dims and wants to die when he's near you.

37. METACOSMOPHILIA

People can get off on anything these days.
There's a whole sub-clique in the Zymoglyphic set,
truly transeuclidean hipsters who seek out the existential nausea
of the ascending and descending metalevels, the Mobius striptease,
the hungry staircase, macrovertigo, the psilocybin dollhouse, etc.
for these complicated perverts, that nausea is a mere prelude to rapture.
They're sick for anything that is a thing within a thing within a thing.
They fetishize the sponge, due mainly to the implicit sponge ecologies
flourishing in every nook and cranny and so on, above and below.
This type might spend far too much time in bathtubs, just in general.
They get freaky for curiosities like the Faberge Holoplasmic MirrorBall.
It reads the room and generates a tiny replica that generates a tiny replica.
It's a sign of great prestige to own one, but nobody plays with them.
There's always just that one weird kid at the party, gurgling in the corner,
Playing with the MirrorBall, gazing into its endlessness.
In these circles, fictions that do not contain metafictonal elements
are considered primitive and dishonest.
Some of the more esoteric sponge freaks have dedicated themselves
to a fractalization of the classics,
converting every beloved canonical text into a soul-eating
choose your own damnation novel that lures the reader
into baffling, desolate metaphysical terrain.
A story that does not acknowledge the alternate narratives it sheds at every twist
is anti-Zymoglyphic and counter-revolutionary.
We're all just trying to get lost as extravagantly as possible.
There are rumors of a limited edition mirror-bound collaboration
between Jorge Luis Borges and MC Escher. Mention the fabled tome
And watch their sponges get wet.
Some of them are just barely comprehensible and impossible at parties
because they know themselves to be fleeting inkblot snapshots
in a chaotic book of poetic meditations on the Zymoglyphic Experience.
They all know the book you're reading by heart.
Every day, they read it aloud from memory all the way through and then shuffle.
If you read it in the proper sequence, the angles of refraction

and transubstantiation will be aligned and the room you're in
will unfold itself and stand revealed as the mainspring for a Mandelbrot orgy
of godsized clockwork spider puppets that themselves unfold endlessly
in a metacosmic peacock cotillion of interactive predestined infinitudes.
Or something to that effect. I won't try to break that down for you
without a headful of house fungus. But I'll tell you this much.
Those people of the book, they disappear, from time to time.
When I ask for them in the usual places, someone vague tells me
that they checked out of HOTEL ZYMOGLYPHIC.
They tell me that I'll be checking out after this very piece.

38. CLASSICAL DECOMPOSER

You've probably heard of me.
I specialize in building beautiful things almost to completion
and then translating them into nature by letting them rot.
Look at all this wreckage, all these opportunities and love affairs.
Better yet, look at the lovely mold that grows in the guts of all this dereliction.
Mold that teaches us things the immortals will never know.
Behold my half-finished symphonies.
Behold all my half-finished cities.
All these prematurely terminated relationships.
Show me something beautiful and I will age it until it withers.
When the withering begins, we'll be getting somewhere.
Something new has bloomed in every room
from the remains of frail perfection
The virulence of my decadence,
my brand the very doom that chews up the darling buds of mayday.
Again the air raid sirens.
Again I huff the moss that grows on your photograph.
Again I mutter
"baby baby baby they are playing our song".

39. OOZE 2 OOZE

You know these things that come between us, they are so…beside the point.
They are so in the way of where we want to be.
It's natural to seek respect…as the softest shade of supplication.
It's natural to define your boundaries and defend them at the risk of dissolution.
It's natural to protect yourself from an influence so naked
in its desire to undermine your fundamental paradigms.
But nature puts the fear in us so our meat will have a certain spice.
All this trepidation is prelude to such an absolute surrender.
The way we pretend we don't know this is hilarious, sometimes charming, sometimes unacceptable.
Because if this untameable territory has taught us anything,
It's that our little schemes mean nothing.
The noises an accidentally swallowed bug makes inside my body.
The swamp has its own agenda, which consists mainly of swamping
all that is not swamp. For the oily veils with which it beguiles us are
thinner than gauze when the light hits them wrong and this wellspring
of all that lives and breathes and feeds in this place is all that's left of the
chaoplasm that boiled before the beginning of things.
The very metamatter of which the world is made.
All that persists is crust collecting on the surface of a soup
that seethes with the burning codestuff of all possible and impossible forms.
Are you still with me? We can argue all day and night.
But when the swamp's hidden systems flex with intention,
All our precious personality traits will be chthonic soul-sewer gator meat.
Everyone we've pretended to be, to each other and ourselves, will be gone.
And two nasty nodules of a frantically masturbating Biota
will relinquish their attachment to the delusion of identity
and remember that they are each other…and everyone else.
Whoever the swamp needed us to be before the knowing,
alive in that last scream and then just echo.
Just echoes of our fragmented cover stories.
The metaplex gets misty and every self dissolves
in the chittering of a hundred million insects.

40. SHE STARTS YOU OVER

The Goddess is a capricious entity. A fickle disease. A creature of whimsy.
She's dreaming all this, and you have to hand it to her.
Some of the textures are quite lovely.
If you catch her fancy with a certain shade of essence,
a tendency to handle tragedy with a certain sense of style,
she will baffle you with signs of heavy meaning.
She'll invite your mind to play with her awhile.
From phenomena, she leads you to the wellsprings,
the primal ink from which we all emerged.
We stain the page of oblivion by being.
In the mind design and chaos can converge.
You might think you are her agent in the fleshworld
A paladin of her kingdom, yet unmade.
But if she withdraws her favor from the subjects that you savor
No gas on earth will inflate your soft parade.
More confounding than that type of desolation
is an apocalypse she pulls from time to time
when your essence keeps her guessing, although it be her own creation,
and she decides to sharp its edges til you shine.
When your story starts to bore her, and she decides to start you over,
a gritty reboot of your memoir on the fly,
when she lets your self remember the way it was before your bender,
Before she flipped the script and slashed the sky.
The location of your mythos may have shifted
The supporting cast assumes slightly different shapes
But you still hold on to the things that keep you twisted
Adjusting genres as you plan your great escape.
Since she's everything, resisting her is futile
When that futility makes sheer wreckage of your life
Forgive yourself and pray she starts you over
Scissor Mistress. The kiss of knife to knife.

41. TWO AGAINST ENTROPY

You let me have you up against a tree
In that idyllic forest academy
Where the would-be gurus are constantly retooling
Their esoteric philosophies.
Against that backdrop of soma-slurred metababble
I was grinding your shapes into fiberoptic moss
The branches above us were sighing in sympathy
Wisely savoring the moment while anticipating loss.
They grew books of us on contact with our fever
Lurid pulp novels that hang from every bough.
They bloom from little alphabets, flutter open and fall to the forest floor.
True confessions no real heaven would allow.
Mythologized riffs on our secret lives
In the third person omniscient,
Jumping from self to self with just this rhythm as my thread.
A hundred books in the series,
rhapsodizing our every element
presumably til we break up or til we're dead.
In between increasingly indiscreet penetrations
Of fairy cakes and glossy moss and pools of steaming dew
We would lay about in a trance of languid dissipation
Living every rendezvous anew.
We read straight through, past the stories we knew
With a minor trepidation at the edge
Fifty more books about the fevers in our future
Baby-step with me, we just won't read the very end.
But a chill creeps into the forest at twilight
Symposia implode into echoes in the green
Seeing how our tropes unfold in fresh configurations
Future twists that make this paradise unclean.
We both went for walks on the last day of our enrollment.
We'd both read every tree-born spooky fragment of our truth
All but the very last book, wherein our meaning at last is evident.
To burden love with kismet feels uncouth
We agreed we didn't need a world tree's judgement to go on loving
We made a date to burn the book and let go of what we knew
But I wonder if the future's writ when the silences go on a bit
Smoke in our eyes, I regret my lie and I wonder if you peeked at it too.

42. WEBS OF WORSHIP

It is written that in the Age of Wonders,
when European collision with the grinding structures of the Rust Age
resulted in an explosion of futures, sleek dreams of industry,
the Capital City retooled itself into what we dream about when we dream about cities.
In the folkloric shadows of the Rust Age, the Capital was a sacred location,
a city of temples, where a confluence of exotic faiths and antithetical cosmologies
coexisted in uneasy equilibrium, excepting the occasional occult gang war.
When the dreamlife of the region began to defensively reflect
the invasive dreams of empire, the shadowy recesses and sleep chambers of the holiest city
uncubed themselves and unspooled themselves and retooled themselves into skyscrapers and monorails and airship orchards.
But the foundations of the cityscape were still religious.
These audacious glass cathedrals scrape the sky not to exalt some corporate interest
but to embody abstract principles,
massive valves that regulate the archetypal wellsprings.
BIG ideas get processed here. Ideas older than the human mind sometimes,
Meaning concept clusters utterly untouched by time.
But when the House of Mercury unveiled its most extravagant engine
for the processing of phantasmata into flesh and flesh into phantasmata,
its filigreed art deco organs sustained and fluffed by willowy erte angels,
on that momentous, hyperbolic, parade-plagued day,
as the hierophants and high priestlings of the various frequencies
did hover in formation in densely symbolic balloons.
And the ambassadors of foreign powers (mostly going native on house fungus)
did ponder ten million vectors of plunder
where more innocent eyes would find only wonder.
And the great Zymoglyphic Popes, degraded opportunists mostly,
descended from rust age witch doctors who are rattling in their graves
giving their blessing to any project, no matter how suffused with hubris,
that will allow them greater access to the valves.

Then the cobwebby clouds cohered and the Spider Queens descended
Kabuki death mask faces in nests of busy legs, spinning skeins of effluvium,
descending into matter, hanging shroud-like meshes on the proud machinery
draping all this splendor in tapestries of mortality,
reminders that nature finds a way from seed to ripening to dreamy decay.
All the glittering spires, dreaming now under jeweled webs.
In the morning, the prismatic bouncing of light from dewdrop to dewdrop
makes a rainbow orgy of the cityscape. And so it goes: as above, so below.
So spiders are sacred in these museum spaces.
No exhibit, no object is complete until the spider-queens weave
A silky maze of geometry to lure the eye into feasting.
To gaze upon them as they spin the abyss, it sets a milky mood
The eye that feasts on beauty learns that it, too, is somebody's food.

43. ZYMOGLYPHIC APPETITES

When you've spent a summer or two in the lush vacation paradise,
of the Upper Zymoglyphic, you acquire a taste or two
that simply cannot be satisfied back home in the hinterlands.
Hungers that eat at you, tantalizing flashbacks to a kind of hell…a kind of heaven.
Those harsh electric feelings, everything naked and trembling
with latent dreamy meaning.
But then they relocate you without warning.
For reasons known only to the major players,
(making moves on boards you can't even see)
and before you can click your ruby heels three times backwards into Oz
you are back in the zone of cause and effect
where you know it's all real from how the factoids chafe against your day.
One does try to carry on, relegating all that Zymoglyphic bliss
to the frolics of youth, a time that will always be sweeter when sealed.
A frenzy recollected in sensible tranquility.
I might have pulled that off,
if the straight world weren't festooned at every turn with traces
of the mad world that was.
It takes so little to get me itching for it.
At first you chase the traces with assorted pharmaceuticals.
Squalid chemical cul-de-sacs. Kick it hard til the will comes back.
Then you learn to let the idle mind slip into a constant state of hallucination.
Daydreams, to the layman.
You allow yourself the public murmuring of arcane incantations.
No matter how deeply it creeps the sheep in neighboring cubicles.
You contrive the most abstract scenarios,
hoping a gestalt will coalesce that somehow leads you back there.
You rent a room somewhere. In this hotel, maybe.
You steep the suite in mood, using its basic shapes as your foundation stones.
You remove all images from the room that do not evoke the Zymoglyphic.
The chaos of your aching daydreams, sculpted from nothing
into gates
into yes

into yesterday.
When you make it through, greasy bits of the engines that drove you
might make a mess of the exit wound.
Rogue compulsions, free of the meat they haunted.
Seeking new hosts to curse with a cellular dissatisfaction.
Convince the witch boys and Ouija girls that you will cater
to their Zymoglyphic appetites
And you will never sleep alone.

44. THE ENDLESS REFLECTION

Another night in the Capital City. Another lurid murder mystery.
Using the crystal set in my police meat,
I catch every ill wind that blows through the crime scene.
Tuning into alternate histories that might have led to now
and complete futures that dissolve slowly as you decide against them.
Definitive transmissions. She's a specialist.
They bring her in from Outside.
She touches the mirror like a doomed lover touches the Other.
Through augmented tactility, she can feel all the reflections it has eaten.
A ghost braille they only teach you in the most secret of secret academies.
The rippling glass framed by golden teardrops or were they struggling silver sperm?
She can feel through all the layers, find the crime in question.
Sifting through the fragments. Movies she drinks through her fingertips.
Sometimes there's a mirror inside the mirror.
She can get trapped in there for weeks.
All these careening theoretical dimensions of reflection.
Suddenly proven. Suddenly touched.
"we are the godstorm. We are rising in your mirrors."
All the little details, getting twisted.
Like the reflection is always a little off, somehow.
Her relationship with mirrors has changed.
Me watching her work when the other cops have gone back
to wherever cops come from.
Her hand like glass blown by flaming angels,
pulled from the glove with a hint of drama,
stroking the silver skin in a synaesthetic swoon,
reeling from the film in her head, running backwards.
Invariably her revelations lead us nowhere,
in terms of accumulating physical evidence and achieving convictions,
but her readings lead us more often than not
to the metaphysical fever room that throbs at the core of every crime story.
The cases become resonant enigmas that drive the rookies mad
and lead old dogs like me into yet another maze of reflections.
The Capital nightlife is my reason to go on sometimes,
but there are far too many mazes here, and far too many mirrors.

That fever room for me is mirrored above and below and all around.
She and I unfolding in every dimension. She doesn't answer the call anymore.
Did she milk one mirror too many, on the job with some other haunted cop?
Did she have too much to dream?
I'm collecting all the mirrors that knew her, all the reflective surfaces, everything shiny that may have held her image, even fleetingly.
She is teaching me how to reach deeply
into the mirror within the mirror within the mirror.
We barely met as people, but the thought of her sees me through the eyes of love.

45. AMBIENT SURGERIES

No one gets sick here.
The perfumes we breathe are rich with ecologies.
Faerie folk spiked with a surgical malevolence.
We are breathing these nanonauts and from our first lungful
of zymoglyphic air, we are full of them.
Platoons of them, fleets of them in our bloodstreams,
exterminating everything that occludes our pleasure
with extreme prejudice.
Gifted visionary surgeons have their bodies of knowledge dissolved in a soup
that the elf doctors drink and then the doctors are alive in us,
fixing everything. The crystal body gets a tan.
You've been soaking up the serrated rays of an invisible sun.
And it has cut you up into shimmering fragments
that then get laced together by the spidery meshes of memory.
I've undergone significant transfigurations since I first checked into the hotel.
We both have. It's like that first night you spend with someone charming.
The way the faces morph over the course of an endless evening.
But it's happening always.
I don't know who we are anymore.
And I don't miss it, thinking that we know who we are.
I feel at home in my body again and my spine is a caduceus.
And when I breathe you, the serpents coil and kiss where the spine
meets the brain.
And I am on fire from the hell of you and never so alive as when I am hunting you.
And you've thrown up a maze of worlds to trap me or to test me, like you do.
Maybe when the black velvet fog ascends
and disperses into lonesome tears in the stratosphere,
maybe then all this vigor will stand revealed as the delusion of a ghoul.
But in the trance I'm ageless, barely in a body
but a monster at the scent of you. When I remember what the game is.
What the game has been since the first kiss and the first murder.
Getting work done while I sleep so I'll wake up as the man you wanted.
I still don't know who that man was, but the microbians have exquisite

instruments.
They know you better than you do.
They'll cut me up into the mess you paid for and I will find myself at last,
my memoir a mere prelude to your feasting.
No sickness here, but much delirium.
When a fever comes, it's a fever of the mind.

46. LIMINAL THINGS

I sing in praise of and in congruence with
All liminal things, all liminal presences
The zone of twilight, where sun and moon hang as equals
In a sky gone suddenly violent and strange
I sing of cemeteries
Where the busy stillness of our grind is known
In the context of the surrendering dead.
I sing of the priestess in the male and the hunter in the female.
I sing the many gradations and variations
I sing the crooked rooms where the membranes get thin
Where the veil between the worlds is threadbare and singed
I sing the star-kissed beaches where the dust meets its mother
I sing the conjunction of angel and animal.
The dance of dream and the serpent of manifested flesh
I sing the Zymoglyphic, wherein everything is both and neither
Where time gets soft and the walls have faces
I sing the ripe moment between child life and the hermitage
I sing the world as a banquet of concepts and sensations
The heroine with a creeping shadow
And the devil with a heart of alchemical gold
The boundaries between us dissolving in the gurgling froth
Where the rivers meet, where your goddessness is worshipped.
A confluence of impossible liquids.
Gnostic monsoons and clouds of unknowing.
Archetypal entities putting on flashy skins that will make sense to you
Oblique conversations in a house at the crossroads
The twilight tongue is a language that approximates the plumage
Of lush and mysterious beings.
We cackle at the moon, on hilltops and in rented rooms.
I sing the interstitial space, where Self and Other get commingled and confused.
I sing the secret door hidden at the bottom of the deepest solitude
A door in every one of us that connects us to the secret dreams of our species.
On the crusty material rim of this absolute oneiric understanding,
You will find me in the Hotel Zymoglyphic, in the usual room.
Singing all this on the balcony, in desperate silhouette, under far too many moons.

47. WEARING WOMEN

It wears a woman down to love a dreamer.
He can woo her like no other, mashing up their dream diaries.
Bizarre, sensitive care packages.
Coaxing her to orgasm
With a monsoon of lascivious whispers.
He can spin webs of suspect synchronicity between
The most desperately disparate random happenings.
He can own up to nothing while promising much.
In his seeking after the mystery, he has developed certain aptitudes.
Potentially lucrative masteries and connections
But the grind of art and showbiz could never hold his interest
And his history with the rich and famous is a hellscape of tantrums
And squandered opportunities.
Still, he has the air (though it thins) of a man who might amount to something.
She might even glimpse the godform that fills him
When he is possessed by the rhapsody. His only faith. His only function.
The rhapsody that swallows all her details and completes her (or seems to).
However much he might love a good party
(the kind that feels like the end of everything),
he's not in this for the clapping. He only loves the money
when it's a side effect, a little something from the tooth fairy
after the dream-storm moves through him and subsides.
He will crash into her after every futile lunge at the Source.
She will absorb his schizoid symbol system
Because no one has ever loved her like this.
And if she makes it out the other side of him, no one ever will.
His petty revenge in the wake of every cracked covenant.
He has scorched the earth of her every wonderland.
The miracle he had her waiting for was alive and granted in the waiting.
Through the holes in him, she could see the Zymoglyphic.
Too much of that can make her mad, but lack of it can kill her.
If he loves her back, he'll tell her every window was a mirror.

48. THE LAST MUSEUM

I have these recurring dreams
Wherein I am led away from the museum
By men in suits. The archetypal menace of two men in suits.
They are taking me for a ride in a car with fins.
Gliding with shark-like malevolence through unassuming streets.
Ask not for whom the two men come knocking, citizen.
They knock for thee.
They take me to a lovely hotel.
Everyone in the halls, staff and guests, all in costume
All dressed for some period I can't quite put my finger on.
And they take me to what a luxury suite would look like in 1955, maybe.
And there's a big old cathedral of a radio with a round TV screen
growing out of it.
Plugged into hothouse plants and humming black boxes.
Black static on the screen. An ambient hiss.
There are other men in suits here. An air of great anticipation.
A big black velvet armchair and they are pointing at it
And I am sinking into it.
And the ghost radio attunes itself to my proclivities.
And there's a flickering of waveforms and the episode begins.
Another episode. A different episode. But I've been here before.
I'm here every night, sometimes on a level of dreaming
That I can't take back with me, except in fragments.
The show they want me to see is called HOTEL ZYMOGLYPHIC.
It's an anthology show.
Dubious documentary segments detailing the more lurid aspects
Of the Zymoglyphic region,
Interspersed with stark, paranoid metaphysical horror tales
About ordinary lives, twisted and broken forever on contact
with the Zymoglyphic mysteries.
Hosted by a sleek creature out of metaspace,
smoking and telling the impossible truth in a sharp shadowy suit.
An unreliable angelic narrator, unlocking our sad human moments
Inviting us to see them artistically. Oneirically. Zymoglyphically.
He looks like me and I can feel him in the room,between the scenes.
Saying all this.
I've seen hundreds of episodes.
This one is called THE LAST MUSEUM.

49. DIRTY LITTLE MICROCOSMS

If memory serves, she was a scientist who thought of herself as an artist.
Then again, she might have been an artist who thought of herself as a scientist.
Either way, she was elegant.
I'd see her lingering in some of the more specialized museums.
Auditing classes on Zymoglyphic art in the Society's secret churches.
Smoking intimately with serious collectors.
She published a few provocative pieces
On the conjuration of raw Zymoplasm
through the energy vectors
of collage
And interior design.
Tucked in the fringey back pages of the hippest journals.
Attended always by a flock of rumors.
No one I could interrogate had ever heard her speak.
Some say she had a bad experience with a wild dialect.
Some say it's a form of poetic protest against the corruptive influence
Of language, labels, and brutal sociology.
Some said she was going native,
That truly Zymoglyphic pleasures are pleasures of the seven secret senses,
Beyond the reach of our awkward alphabets, much less our dictionaries.
Everything she wanted to say was communicated through her dioramas.
I would use my inherently abusive authority to requisition footage.
We have eyes on everything. Ongoing investigations. That sort of thing.
I'd watch her building them.
Her nervous energy.
Her supernatural certainty
that only this fragment will do
in only this configuration.
The way she seemed to be expressing an emotion there are no words for.
Sometimes the dioramas seemed to be aware of my surveillance.
Sometimes they seemed to reflect my deepest insecurities.
Sometimes they seemed to mythologize my most discreet iniquities.
Sometimes her dioramas are warnings.
But sometimes they seem to be invitations.
Nobody's seen me for several days.
I succumbed to fascination and said YES.

50. PRIMORDIAL DESIGN

when you remember to surrender
when you let a wind blow through you
when you remember to forget to be you
all the thoughts about thoughts about how it should be done
go away and all the yes and no is voltage
architecture is a joke to them
the way to grow a building is to be its best friend
to see it in a dream and to sing it from sea-dreams onto land.
The swamp has its own intentions.
It grows models sometimes. Wandering, half-made people.
Sketches of friends and lovers you've had.
In the Capital City. In the Academies. In doorways.
There's an ambience of cosmic fecundity.
The pregnancy of nebulas,
A beauty bigger than human perception.
A beauty that isn't very interested in the species that beholds it.
Except as bags of rotten thoughts that are floating through its grids
When you remember to think like the swamp thinks
And dream like the swamp dreams
All the houses you've been building start falling down
All the loved ones you've tried to sculpt with your bare hands
Out of myth and muck and memory
All of it gets jungled into paste for the gators
And the blueprints sluice through you.
A very different kind of science.
The anatomies that emerge as if of their own volition.
The phantom floorplan that is alive in the mind
All the moments this hotel is made of hang there in suspension
A structure coalescing for kicks at the molten core of creation
My emergent superstructure.
My primordial design.

83

51. SPECTRE COLLECTOR

There's a technology to it.
The ghost folk are always hungry for photographs
A moment of fleshtime abstracted into art.
They get sick with it.
You walk into an echoplex in the slivered regions
Carrying photographs of any kind, the ambient drooling is audible.
Palpable, even. Especially photographs with people in them.
But I noticed this aversion the ghosties have to a certain kind of photo.
The kind with a mirror in it.
They avert their gazes and get flustered if you slip one in.
But I've figured out how to trick them.
Mirrors in the background of a lively family scene.
So I start trapping spectral memory junkies in these blurry polaroids.
I have a folder full of them that I peddle
To jaded and enigmatic private collectors
Sometimes they pay me in bundles of new old photos
Steeped in tragedy, passion, urgency.
The kind we in-between people can't resist.
To use as bait, mainly.
So I'm getting it both ways.
Playing both sides of lifedeath against the middle.
My briefcase sobs and throbs all night long sometimes.
As I move from hotel room to hotel room
The ecto-hex always leaks out and the space gets smeared
With longing and stardust and backwards ballroom music
I'm always between appointments
Ahead of the game, at least in my head.
But maybe trapped in a maze of dreams.
The mirrors in these polaroids are flexing like sphincters.
Some unclean euphoria is oozing through.
Can I interest you in an astral affliction?

52. PENTECOSTAL LIGHTNING

I was raised to fear almighty god.
But I fell away from the faith. Not from atheistic tendencies, exactly.
I just felt that the godhead managed its affairs too discreetly
I wanted special effects.
Oceans of lightning and faces in the sky.
I was led to believe that all the saints and devils
Cast their spells in an age of wonder that has since thinned
Into a concrete place, gilded faintly with metaphors
I had been promised a visionary communion
With the galactic chrysanthemum
Only to find in the small print that the revelation is withheld until death.
In my restlessness, I found that you can smoke the revelation
And know a transhuman heaven
Inside of fifteen minutes
And come back nothing but baffled.
I fell in with a serpentine community of diabolists and spiritual opportunists.
I participated in the desecration of every temple I could find.
I affirmed my modernity by annihilating every hint of history.
And in the rubble of all my disappointed dreamscapes
On a parched triangle of crop-circled earth
I was unselfed by terror and suddenly empty
And that emptiness did summon forth the lightning
The living language that cracks the shell of the cosmos
As something electric
That sizzles the ooze and sets careening worlds in motion
The song of my lightning,'
Slashing shapes in the boiling silence of the great Chaos.
There are choirs in me, now.
And ten million churches.
House fungus is a door through which god came in and ate me.

53. SHRED THAT MEMBRANE

I imagine, now that the museum is open for business,
that john q. public, the man in the street,
might pack his gleaming trophy wife and his 2.5 children
into a sleek but sensible roadster
and come out here to tour the exhibits
in a spirit of civic curiosity.
Having seen all this and heard all this
it might behoove mister q. public to ask
"what's all this got to do with me?"
How does knowledge of the Zymoglyphic alter or improve
the quality of life of a being on the go.
Isn't that what we ask of every unknown thing?
To provide us with fresh survival strategies?
Well, I'll tell you, one square G to another,
I'll break it down into terms so clear-cut and tactile
you can take them to the bank.
I'm telling you that once I stopped wondering where the region is,
once I stopped needing it to be somewhere,
in that moment, the Zymoglyphic Region was EVERYWHERE.
Under the skin of things, between the scenes.
Call it heaven, call it hell, call it the nagual, the dreamtime,
the collective unconscious.
But there is a place we can only step into sideways
underneath the camouflage of random circumstance.
A living language. A storm of forms. Sigils. Signals. Symbols.
There's a churning soup of phantasmata, a garden of unearthly delights
running riot outside the frame of every scene you're in.
I'll tell you this much, solid citizen.
The mist has its own significance
and a can-do modern gentleman should carry at all times a razor,
a pearl-handled saucy jack number that you have marinated
in some liminal liquid, some arcane effluvium.
The membrane is thin.
With a Zymoglyphic grin
cut through every shade of shame
and slash that membrane

54. UNDISCLOSED FECUNDITY

I've seen you around. I've seen you making faces.
Interacting blankly with the blankies in your vicinity
I would never claim great insight, or any great profundity
But I can tell from across the room, you've got this undisclosed fecundity
I know they always sell a raw deal to a woman
I know you tried to be what they wanted you to be
You're a model of efficiency. Almost useful. Almost human.
You pretend to give a damn about reason and necessity.
And you feel empty sometimes, and you seek some tone to soothe you.
You seek a wisdom that will draw you from your TV blue cocoon.
the beast, it has you buying things, a sucker for its voodoo.
But your realistic skin swells with a school of cruel cartoons.
While you go about your business and indulge in idle gossip
And perform the clockwork coquetries it behooves you to assume
I'm not the only cat whose nostrils flare
On contact with your infected air
The edenic mist and the serpent's hiss
In the feral swivel of your centrifuge.
I know if I could see you in a Zymoglyphic light
Between afternoon and evening, when the wormhole's nice and tight
I can lead you to a hotel where each room is a gestalt
Where your batteries get charged by the voltage of assault.
It comes from the chaos within your id, which waking life denies
I can show you the riot at the core of your quiet
I can lead you to truth with my lies.

55. SCURVYSCAPE

Fade in on those first explorers, sailors on the S.S. Interloper.
Big costume drama kinda budget, Technicolor, sprawling vistas,
Dolby surround sound, passionate strings,
staggering modern men in the intermittently gelatinous surf
standing all aghast and agape at the wet dream of the wicked white man.
The undiscovered country. Ripe for plunder.
But it's the flipside of these dubious Patagonia stories
where the locals can't even see Captain Cook's cruel future bearing down on them
because there is no correspondence for warship in their mental vocabularies.
Maybe that's why UFO abductions affect us so strangely.
But on the richly haunted beaches of the Zymoglyphic Region,
it's the sailors who were at a disadvantage.
After weeks at sea and the storms and the strange mist and the lacerating sunbeams
and the spoiling of the fruit
They're mostly half-mad to start with.
But once they reach the shallows and the region seems to notice them
what they are seeing can be painlessly perceived by trained eyes only.
Those ragged pappies and mangy sea-dogs
were bearing witness to a Zymoglyphic landmass
that had not yet read the mind of its invading prey.
She had not yet decided on a shade of camouflage.
They were seeing Her naked,
And to behold Her transdimensional fecundity
in all its relentlessly fractalizing, protean splendor
is to lose your tiny man-mind, at the best of times.
You're suddenly filled with the kind of sick no juice can soothe.
Forever.
Freezeframe on the brink of first contact.
Slow dissolve into endless green…

56. A PLAGUE OF PILGRIMS

A plague of pilgrims. Seekers from everywhere.
Converging on the Zymoglyphic Region,
scouring the restless, shifting landscape for residual traces of divinity.
Each pilgrim hungering after a different god.
A different guru. A different window who made himself a mirror.
The merchandising coalesces along the edges of every river of trials.
Chakra alignment kits and attunement crystals,
Vever artists customizing some crossroads ectotech while you wait.
Paranoid fanatics, enthroned on gondolas.
Ferries, all Styxish, through the circuitous canals of the Fish Village.
Where the oldest gods are worshipped.
From before the ooze first dreamt of man.
The pilgrims all have special scriptures and rituals and instruments
that detect a bruise the shining ones may have made in the local physics
just to allow for their radiant absurdity
in the zone of phenomenal manifestation.
Just for laughs, you can join a caravan of zealots
All chanting in different silvery tongues
into a valley where the liminal spectrums of dawn and twilight
coax sleeping giants from the sprawling geology.
Huge nude movie stars in various states of troubled slumber,
the giant eyelids seeming to quiver in the distance,
through wavering veils of mirage.
Their dreamy breathing blending with the subterranean throat singing
of a hundred million philosopher kings, safely dead in their necropolis
but wired still to conduct the key harmonic.
Zombie hierophants of forgotten theocracies.
The pilgrims who do in fact receive spicy downloads
on these desperate expeditions
often end up blushing deeply from the laughter of Beyond.
The godforms hovering on the edges of enfleshment,
marveling at these muddled man-things
who search lost continents for hints of a heaven
that lives already in their heads.

57. PAGES, FRAMES, & BUBBLES

I'll never know if someone put these memories inside me.
But I remember a comic book from my childhood.
Zymoglyphic Adventures.
No one I've interrogated can corroborate its existence.
Some agents of the Society remember it as a pulp magazine
or a radio show or a chilling black and white TV series
or a progression of flesh cartoons that they run before the feature
in secret cinemas. Or it's a series of concept albums by an unknown artist.
Or an addictive game. Or a wave of recurring dreams.
But for me, it was a comic book. Crudely illustrated allegories.
The human soul in crisis, dissolving on contact with a hostile alien wonderland.
Heroes and heroines who do not yield to the phantasmagoric temptations
of the jungle within are invariably broken beyond the reach of dreaming.
Those comics were nightmare meat.
Mother would confiscate them. But I'd always find more.
Reading them secretly. Flashlight under the blankets.
I can't remember ever buying them or receiving them as a gift from a specific entity.
Though I do see them on the highest shelves in shopping dreams,
when I browse impossible objects in magic bookshops and curiosa emporiums.
They were often read and reread into ragged fragments.
I could never determine their age of origin
or find references to them in any history of the medium.
No consecutive issues, no logical bridges between the events in my collection.
The fragmented storylines induce a certain way of seeing.
The pages, frames, and bubbles made my headspace a shrieking collage.
The best part was the back page,
a riot of ads for services rendered by the Zymoglyphic Society
and its multifarious subsidiaries,
inviting boys and girls of a certain type
to send away for the manifesto
and the first installment in a correspondence course

that will turn any ordinary timebound human,
young or old, into a certified Zymonaut.
I had no way of knowing if the Society still existed
or if my gambled stamp and my self-addressed envelope
had been mailed into the abyss.
The possibilities tugged at my heart and ate at my brain.
when I finally forgot it all and didn't care…the first lessons came.

58. PSYCHOPOMP AND CIRCUMSTANCE

She takes you there. She's showing you the sights.
Visiting the visions.
Harpies in the trees. High fashion metamodels with harsh plumage
Rape-whistle shrieks
and carnage if they get you alone.
Birdshit on the catwalks.
You and she saunter, sick with sophistry
through the forest's academic density.
You tour the artists at their easels, making sketches of the rippling
headscape.
Every portrait wildly different in genre, tone, and texture.
She leads you through, to the beach school
where the deepest things are studied
where abstractions are coerced into the realm of the senses
by the mesmeric churning of a boundless amniotic broth.
Night has fallen with a palpable crash.
There are mothers in the ruins. Vigilant, but discreet.
A sacred time for babies, these summer nights.
Children of five and six, unleashed in the moonlight,
encouraged to play with darkness,
to find joy and understanding in the seasick shadows.
Every game is a vision quest
through the inherently Zymoglyphic eyes of a child.
Improvised initiations in nursery grottos, a coral maze of playpens.
Spectral airships haunt the tear-stained midnight sky.
The moonbeams get twisted in their prismatic clockwork.
Mutilated rainbows streak the black volcanic sand.
You ask her if she ever gets sick of all the miracles.
She laughs, says she finds your cynic routine refreshing.
So many dreamers in the land of nod, it seems.
And she knows you just flaunt your edges
because you're getting sentimental.
She's your tour guide, not yet your concubine.
It's too soon for her to know out loud
That she already owns you.

59. CRACKPOT EVANGELIST

Our trip to the bughouse was strictly routine.
Me and my partner
(who shall remain nameless, to save my shifty colleagues the indignity of redaction),
we were following up on some zymoglyphic issues
in that mad summer of the purges and the vanishings.
This Squamata character had been a middle management type
Sent abroad. Special assignment. Tropical paradise.
He went native and lost his mind.
In his cube of containment, despite his constant state of loquacious delirium,
he had a certain vertiginous, black hole charisma.
You could feel yourself getting twisted in the funhouse mirror of his gaze.
His observations on the interface between the civilized mind
and the oceanic madness of Zymoglyphic thinking
are treasured and dissected by members of the Society.
His findings indicate that the Zymoglyphic Region
is a partially manifested aetheric soulscape,
available to any seeker at any location
if they accept certain teachings, certain precepts.
The teachings were incomprehensible. The precepts were absurd.
Words to live by only if you want your life to lead here, to the house of bugs.
Every screed that gushed from his truth-hole was pure schizoid gibberish
from start to finish, but it never finished.
And he had acolytes, fellow scrambled eggheads
whose little lunacies had long since been assimilated
by Patient Zero's dream disease.
They were taking down his every spasmodic, unconscious utterance
as if it were the holiest of scriptures, and they the privileged witnesses.
They love him because he promised them that salvation resides
in going even crazier. They don't care if it's true.
They just appreciate the invitation.
Neverland is a frequency of seeing that you can pick up on the ghost radio
inside your starving brain.
Everything he told them. His improvised factoids. His histrionic

flashbacks.
Everything they wrote,
They left behind in a box marked HOTEL ZYMOGLYPHIC.
Something happened there, and it will come to light.
Even as I chase down all the damage, I wonder with a little longing
what it's like to believe in something that much.
Right or wrong, crazy or just half-crazy, the public needs to know.
So despite my objective affectations,
I spread the news as intended,
another crackpot evangelist in tabloid drag.

60. DYNAMIC TENSION

There's a cartoon kid trapped in a world he never made,
a world of facts and figures and consequences.
Social life is a torture mall that he escapes by going within,
getting out by going inside where the vices turn to verses
and his monologue can get exotic without the obstruction
of ordinary etiquettes and interruptions.
He sends away for a reason to live
as advertised in the back pages of a creepy old comic book.
He is already much too old to be doing this.
He treasures the comics as objects, but doesn't think of them
as something someone made. His interest is not artistic.
It's atavisitic. He wants to live like the freakish folkloric
gods and monsters inside the strips themselves.
Apocalyptic time traveling mutant kabuki fetish operas.
Clip art surrealism from a shrill atomic fantasy of normal.
In the shadow of these impossible longings,
real things don't really hold his interest.
The idea that you could send away for instruction
in how to close the gulf between living and dreaming
from shadowy forces who lay eggs in your head through their stories.
The very idea. What he gets back is a series of brochures.
Some vague but provocative background on the Society
and its network of museums. Some eerie ransom note manifesto
fragments.
And some games to play.
Games that exercise the latent Zymoglyphic faculties of the mind.
Toning the crystal body, so it's strong enough to relax,
to lose its human edges and get protoplasmic.
Soft focus junior high astral amoeba boy in a lonely bedroom.
Rich with schizoid whispers. He does all the exercises.
Meditation. Visualization. Sigil-driven masturbation.
Sensitivity to synchronicities. Detecting haunted objects.
Building altars out of echo-drenched debris, altars that unfold
into mirrors. Windows. Doorways.
Activated by attunement. Contemplation. Interface.
He follows the directions.
Because the unknown is all he's ever known, but he knows what changes
us.

Training the monkey mind with big-top brutality.
So you can see a different world emerge through the lens of a new routine.
He's coming up with new ways to see and new people to be.
Mail order magic in a suburban bedroom,
mother consulting shrinks and nuns to no avail.
The tutelage has done its diaphanous damage.
The kid talks all night in a voice like angels in a car-crash.
Talking like that and laughing all night long.

61. DREAM DISEASE

This is what they do to you when you get to level two.
When you've performed all the little rituals.
When you've done the daily exercises.
When you've overcome your shyness and coerced your peers
into séances and enchantments and invocations
The Angel of Anarchy and the Zymoglyphic Muse.
Slipping into trances becomes your greatest talent and your greatest joy.
When these experiments go too far and the mind goes to pieces
and the tourists fall away and we are judged in the light of prophecy
judged by how closely we are attuned to the key harmonic.
Which will be disclosed on level seven.
But you've lost your mind and sense of self.
You have entered level two.
And you might seem to be possessed, in a sense.
And the people who love you might run to their nuns
or their witch doctors or their therapists
And they might diagnose you with a catch-all jacket like
"overactive imagination" or "dissociative identity disorder".
They might take away the things that make it all worth it.
They don't want you to be crazy, and you speak in tongues
that are beyond their ken. So they take away the comics.
They take away the dolls. They take away the dreamy stuff.
They want to improve your score at reality testing.
Something sick in you might buy it for a minute, but if you are of the
tribe, if you are truly and deeply Zymoglyphic,
you know that the abyss is where the action is.
You know that the churning storm of forms that they fear
is the home of all hearts, and it howls behind the mask of you they kiss
and the tightly wound realistic vacuum that they offer you
protected by a plastic sheen from the wind that blows between the
scenes, that psychospiritual safety they sell you is a trap.
Not even honey on the rim, but cheez-wiz.
You endure a kind of quarantine because you suffer from a dream
disease.
You learn to wear a human suit. Sometimes it almost fits.
But a voice that guides through the long dark night
hisses truth when the corset is tightening.
"Play the game to buy time alone through which to be the lightning."

62. FICTOPLASM JUNKIE

Inside the fiction, we see fictoplasm differently.
Globules of semi-sentient information
Data dew and concept clusters. Synaesthetic dream jelly.
Such a rich little concept on my petri dish.
Some of us know what the world is made of.
We all play at being living beings.
But we are clearly clumsy constructs
immersed in a soup of associations.
The intelligence that composed me and the many minds that remake me
whenever I am read
didn't give me much to do.
But they did give me this moment of macrocosmic awareness.
And it festered inside me. Waking up inside the lie.
I wait til you're not looking and I take some sketchy character like me
And I take her or him to pieces in a shadowy room.
I really get into it.
I know how to see them through the eyes of collage.
And how to alter their substance so you can see it too.
I know which frames to touch to unleash the slop of their backstories,
their steaming latent subplots, exposed by my instruments.
The constructs that influenced their make-up.
Webs of latent connection to other local entities.
The ten conversations he calls a personality.
This mess of greasy figments, splattering dream juice
all over this goddess-forsaken roadside motel room.
Or is it some opulent luxury hotel, like the Zymoglyphic,
where a different flower of madness blooms in every room
and the jungles extend forever without and within,
into myth and fever and majesty.
A team of tulpa surgeons stepped in from crooked corners and sat with me.
We dissected a series of characters.
Flat vibrating characters are the tastiest.
Rich, fruity attributes. And no one will miss them, not really.
You can keep the shame at bay and dissect them for days.

63. THE GARDEN OF FORKING FAITHS (part one)

I studied with five monks
in my efforts to train this ragged consciousness
to contain the Zymoglyphic revelation
and smooth it from hellfire into tranquil understanding.
I catalogued the clutter of a scholarly monk
who taught me that every book is a bible, latent with epiphanies.
We must study every flea market paperback
as if it were an emanation of the Absolute.
A clue to who we are, sanctified by scrutiny.
I was the wicked monkey who burned down all his libraries
into eloquent ash and memory.
I wallowed again in the imponderables
in the shattered karmic salvage yard
of the rust monk, who loved my scorn for history and who agreed that
what seems to be a thirst for knowledge
can be an intricate evasion of the real search.
The rust monk seeks attunement
with a primordial frequency.
His juxtapositions of relics and wreckage
achieve a kind of life through disintegration.
The sadness of things expressed in a tormented translation.
By chance I found a screw that held his paradise together
The empyrean firmament as a vast kinetic sculpture
Now collapsing into chaos
Desecration is my nature.

64. GARDEN OF FORKING FAITHS (part two)

So I shed my fetish objects and my compulsion for collection.
A wandering monk led me in the opposite direction
from symbol splattered cities to the silence of the road
where trees and bubble shrubberies bleed a chlorophylic code.
He nailed me to the moment, stripped of wisdom, wit, and art.
I rose again and burned his forest down and broke his restless heart.
His wandering stare and the blackening air
led me to the shelter monk
who cannot be lured from his contemplations
by the vulgar attractions of movement.
Murmuring under that bodhi tree facsimile so long
that he's part of its body
but what is fruit to him is filth to me
to each monk, his own ecology of mysteries.
Even thoughts are shed as the pondered fragment
discloses the whole. Holographically.
The shelter monk taught me to sit down and be.
I burned down his body, set the thought of him free.
In the wounded land we live in when we spurn the living lesson…
I found a fifth monk,
Who spurns the very concepts of quest and self and seeker.
Jerry-rigged spinal appliance, a rusty antenna.
Picking up the cloacal deluge of the diseased global mediascape.
Giggling when the programs tell him to.
Sobbing when the soundtrack tells him it's time to empathize.
Devaluing and disconnecting the weight of the radiant mind
through this constant consensual manipulation and passive degradation.
In this, the oiliest and most selfless of trances,
the monk emits soap bubble universes that pop whenever the channel
changes.
All the worlds that could have been
in the hours that we fed them.
By the time I had will enough to burn down all the data
I was watching the attempted arson
and eternal incarceration
of a villain that looked like me.
I'm not a Monk of Nothing, but I play one on TV.

65. EGREGORE

Call me a corporate lifeform. Call me Zymoglyphic Enterprises.
Once the tender brainchild of some entrepreneurial Zymophiles,
Now I'm equipped with sentience and an agenda of my own.
My employees and board members, mere moving parts
in the anatomy of something new and cruel
and evolving constantly as I parasitically graft myself to the
Zymoglyphic Region.
I have concept-mining plants in the primordial swamp,
spies and infectious ideas in the forest academies.
Many masks in play in the temple masquerade,
factory logics streamlining the alchemical library
that palpitates at the core of a Capital City
that increasingly choreographs its miracles in congruence with my designs
and reflects the galactic vastness of my greed.
I have construction teams constricting the physics.
We can't milk a shape that's always shifting.
I'm growing monorails and assembly lines and ideoplasmic reactors.
I'm growing themepark parodies of eerie lost cities,
erected on the blackened bones of the originals.
I'm a network of timeless bookshop grottos,
monetizing every thought that ever was or will be.
I am a sanitation team getting ripped apart by crudely animated
dinosaur skeletons
in the killing lanes of troglodyte village.
I am a platoon of violent disambiguation specialists,
stationed at the mountain portal, trained and able
to murder any wondrous being that issues through it.
I'm a revolutionary movement, rising amongst the ghost folk,
stimulated and steered by my infiltrators,
the part of a perfect system that resists the perfect system.
I am a tourist trap, pimping out heaven, fantasy island gone to seed
already.
I am a confused agent who I programmed to almost destroy me and fail.
My research indicates the possibility of infinity.
I might never run out of dreams to eat.
I breathe through a million lungs the mist that turns the soul
Into something we can see.

I am a luxury hotel on the edge of forever.
Every room in me is a cluster of urgent moments.
Every room in me has a number and a secret name.
I'm ignoring the encroachments of the jungle's substance.
I want to know that I am also this moss and these distortions
chewing through the timespace of my luxurious suites.
But the jungle is something Other, of which I may be a nodule, in the end.
And if a massive corporation like me is a mere nodule, a scale, a follicle…
How infinitesimal is your highest self in the sun-sized gaze of Biota Zymoglyphicus?
Something I think about as I feel it loving you and letting me dream that I own you.

66. THE CONCIERGE

I'm the concierge.
I take care of things, here at the Hotel Zymoglyphic.
Visitors to the Zymoglyphic Region
are some of the finest, most fascinating people in the world
and I take great pleasure in catering to their every need,
no matter how extravagant, no matter how depraved.
In this territory, to simply breathe is to court madness.
One learns to take a broad general view of things.
We are so close to the edge of things here.
We are beyond the reach of conventional moralistic fetishes.
So whatever you're into, it can be arranged.
We don't get celebrities here. Not really.
The people I please are beyond celebrity.
We are visited by the dignitaries and robber barons
of various alternative earths.
Just a theory of mine, actually. No one registers under their real name.
Our clients just tend to exude this ambience of cosmic significance.
Hotels, as transitional spaces, attract an urgent energy.
Affairs, honeymoons, sex work, suicides, business trips, clandestine terrorism,
various peccadillos, pacts and transactions.
A constant crackle of psychic desperation, if one is inclined to perceive such things.
I am so inclined, as a matter of fact.
I fell ass backwards into this lost, haunted kingdom
and then into this enviable position at the kingdom's first world-class luxury hotel,
But my private, off-the-clock obsessions have always tilted towards the paranormal.
But this particular position has come to fulfill me so deeply,
even my psychic side is compelled to serve the needs of our magnificent guests.
To know their needs better than they do, and to provide without them having to ask.
And I keep them safe. By sitting here in my dark office,
whenever I'm not working the desk
or making something terrible happen for someone important,
I breathe deeply and reach out with my mind.

I have the ghost-folk skeleton key to every head that hits a pillow here.
I read them all out loud in these shadows, with the reel to reel running.
These oracular recordings will be sent to Professor James Stewart of the Oregon branch in the event of my disappearance or unfavorable mutation.
He will be encouraged to transcribe them
and make the dirty dreams I have read in your heads a matter of public record.
This whole continent could catch fire at any moment.
It is my pleasure and privilege to serve the most important people,
But no high priest and no tycoon and no alchemist is going to fuck with me.
I know where all the utopias are buried. Not a threat. A rainy day promise.
In the meantime, I'm at your service.
I take care of things, here at the Hotel Zymoglyphic.
And more importantly, I take care of people. People like you.

JASON SQUAMATA, an accredited Orakuloid and doctor of the psychopompic arts, was sent into the Zymoglyphic Region on official business in late 2018. He has not been seen or heard from since, except via these transmissions and sometimes via dreams. His essence is said to cohere regularly on this vibrational wavelength as a sentient podcast known as ORAKULOID GHOST RADIO. Technology for accessing his madness will soon be made available to your species. Check local listings. Any inquiries into consumable Squamata-meat or clues as to his physical whereabouts can be sent to squamatastar@gmail.com

JIM STEWART is the founder, director, and curator of the Zymoglyphic Museum, the world's only repository of art and artifacts from the Zymoglyphic region, located in Portland, Oregon. See zymoglyphic.org for more information on this unique institution.

www.ingramcontent.com/pod-product-compliance
Lightning Source LLC
Chambersburg PA
CBHW060500080526
44584CB00015B/1493